Animal Planet

Chihuahuas

RICHARD MILLER WITH DIANE MORGAN

Chihuahuas

Project Team
Editor: Stephanie Fornino
Copy Editor: Ellen Bingham
Interior Design: Leah Lococo Ltd. and Stephanie Krautheim
Design Layout: Tilly Grassa

T.F.H. Publications
President/CEO: Glen S. Axelrod
Executive Vice President: Mark E. Johnson
Publisher: Christopher T. Reggio
Production Manager: Kathy Bontz

T.F.H. Publications, Inc.
One TFH Plaza
Third and Union Avenues
Neptune City, NJ 07753

Discovery Communications, Inc. Book Development Team
Maureen Smith, Executive Vice President & General
    Manager, Animal Planet
Carol LeBlanc, Vice President, Marketing and Retail
    Development
Elizabeth Bakacs, Vice President, Creative Services
Peggy Ang, Director, Animal Planet Marketing
Caitlin Erb, Marketing Associate

 Exterior design ©2006 Discovery Communications, Inc. Animal Planet, logo and Animusings are trademarks of Discovery Communications, Inc., used under license. All rights reserved. *animalplanet.com*

Interior design, text, and photos ©2006 T.F.H. Publications, Inc.

Printed and bound in China
07 08 09 10   3 5 7 9 8 6 4 2

ISBN 9-78 0793-83754-0

Library of Congress Cataloging-in-Publication Data

Miller, Richard, 1942-
   Chihuahuas / Richard Miller.
      p. cm. — (Animal Planet pet care library)
   ISBN 0-7938-3754-5 (alk. paper)
   1. Chihuahua (Dog breed) I. Animal Planet (Television network) II. Title. III. Series.
   SF429.C45M56 2006
   636.76—dc22   2006007719

This book has been published with the intent to provide accurate and authoritative information in regard to the subject matter within. While every precaution has been taken in preparation of this book, the author and publisher expressly disclaim responsibility for any errors, omissions, or adverse effects arising from the use or application of the information contained herein. The techniques and suggestions are used at the reader's discretion and are not to be considered a substitute for veterinary care. If you suspect a medical problem consult your veterinarian.

The Leader In Responsible Animal Care For Over 50 Years!™

www.tfh.com

Table of Contents

Chapter 1

Why I Adore My
Chihuahua

The Chihuahua is a delightful toy dog to know, own, and love. In fact, people have come to adore the Chihuahua for a variety of reasons, including his small size, feisty temperament, intelligence, coat types and color range, longevity, and ability to live in a small space with minimal exercise requirements.

Origin of the Chihuahua

The Chihuahua is an old breed whose origins can be traced at least back to ancient Mexico. But much is shrouded in mystery, and there are dozens of different stories about the breed's origins. One such story asserts that the Chihuahua was the sacred dog of the Aztecs. Another claims that the original owners of the Chihuahua were Toltecs, who called this dog Techichi. However, other experts state firmly that the Techichi was some sort of rodent, not a dog at all. At any rate, we do know that the name actually comes from the city Chihuahua (not the other way around), which is located in the beautiful Sierra Madre mountains.

Whatever the history of the breed is, it is not a completely happy one. We know that this tiny dog was once sacrificed by priests during religious rituals and that yellow and red Chihuahuas were regularly killed when their owners died—not from sentiment but because it was believed that the dog would take on the sins of his master after death. Blue dogs, however, were considered sacred. Montezuma II, the last Aztec ruler, supposedly kept hundreds of Chihuahuas in his palace. And Santa Ana, the Mexican dictator who sold part of Mexico to the United States, had a large number of them. In fact, his Chihuahuas supposedly accompanied him into battle, and they were found in his camp when he was finally defeated and captured.

The breed was accepted into the American Kennel Club (AKC) in 1904, and the first registered Chihuahua was appropriately named Midget. Chihuahuas really started to become

The Chihuahua comes in two coat varieties: smooth and long.

popular in the United States around 1850, when about two dozen of the breed were imported into the country. Others were sold to American tourists in Mexican border towns. Nearly all present-day Chihuahuas can trace their ancestry back to these dogs.

Physical Characteristics

The Chihuahua is the world's smallest dog. However, his small stature hides the heart of a lion. This dog's compact size, in addition to a beautiful, varied coat and long life span, makes him a truly unique breed.

Coat Varieties

The Chihuahua comes in two coat varieties: smooth and long. The smooth-coated Chihuahua has a hard, smooth coat, usually with an undercoat. The long-coated variety has long hair, especially on the ears, the back of the front legs, around the neck, and on the tail; he also has a nice long set of pants (long hair from his tail to his hocks that creates the look of pants or culottes). The long coat can range from a few sparse long hairs to very heavily coated.

Pet buyers should not be alarmed if they find a litter of puppies that has both varieties present. One could find both varieties in a litter if one parent is long coated and the other smooth or if both parents are smooth. A mixed litter of puppies is genetically impossible from two long-coated parents.

Coat variety is purely a decision of

The Expert Knows

Where in the World Did the Chihuahua Originate?

Some experts believe that the Chihuahua originally came from China, while others suggest Malta, Egypt, or the Sudan. Did this dog come across the Bering Strait with ancient humans, or was he transported here on ancient Chinese or Mediterranean sailing vessels? Or did he arise from the hairless breeds of South America? Unless DNA testing clears up the issue, the Chihuahua's origins will remain an interesting puzzle.

preference. An animal of either variety should have the same physical appearance except for the coat.

Color

The Chihuahua can be any color or color pattern, which obviously allows for a great deal of variety. Sometimes you might hear of a Chihuahua being advertised as a rare color. However, no color can accurately be described as rare, really, since they are all available. If you are seeking a particular color, it may be difficult to find it in the general area where you live. But that does not mean it is rare, just that you have to look elsewhere for it.

Famous Chihuahua Owners

The pop-opera star Enrico Caruso owned a pack of Chihuahuas. Other famous Chihuahua owners include or included Paula Abdul, Paris Hilton, Jayne Mansfield, and Marilyn Monroe.

Many people think of Chihuahuas as having only tan variations. Nothing could be further from reality. The present-day Chihuahua can be seen in any color pattern known in canines, which even includes merle patterns (bluish or reddish gray mixed with black patches). The bottom line is that true to the AKC standard, the Chihuahua can be any color—solid, marked, or splashed.

Some colors have eye rims and nose leathers that are chocolate colored, self or flesh colored, or gray. All of these pigments are acceptable for breeding or showing.

Eye color can also be varied, with colors ranging from nearly black to ruby red. I have seen one Chihuahua who had one dark brown eye and one china blue eye. This condition is not a fault per the AKC breed standard.

Head

The Chihuahua's head is truly a unique feature of the breed. In fact, no other breed uses the term "apple-domed skull" in its breed standard. The head is rounded from the point where the muzzle joins the skull (stop) over the top to where the skull meets the neck (occiput). The skull should appear rounded from ear to ear. Some Chihuahuas also have what is called a "molera," which is a soft spot in the skull. This characteristic is acceptable in the breed.

The ears should appear large, but they should not be out of proportion to the head. The muzzle should be slightly pointed, never broad or flat.

Life Span

Chihuahuas live long lives. In fact, it is not unusual to hear of a dog who lived well into his teens. One of the reasons for such a long life span is that the breed has nearly no life-threatening diseases to which it is genetically predisposed.

Proportion

The Chihuahua should not look as if he is standing on stilts, and he should not appear long like a Dachshund. The standard calls for a dog who is slightly off-square. "Slightly" is not defined, but it is my opinion that neither tall nor long could fit this description.

Size

You may have heard stories of the tiny Chihuahua who never grew to be even 1 pound (0.5 kg) in weight. This may be true, but in the nearly 50 years that I have known the breed, I have never seen such an animal. A tiny, healthy six-week-old puppy will usually weigh about 20 ounces (0.6 kg). Given that the Chihuahua should not be weedy or spindly in appearance, claims of mature dogs weighing less than 1 pound (0.5 kg) are probably only claims. The other end of the weight spectrum probably has no limit. I have seen dogs who tipped the scale at well over 10 pounds (4.5 kg).

With the two extremes given, you might be wondering what the Chihuahua's ideal weight is. My answer as a breeder, judge, and devoted lover of the breed would be an animal of at least 4 pounds (1.8 kg) and less than 6 pounds (2.7 kg). A Chihuahua may not exceed 6 pounds (2.7 kg) and compete in the show ring. Generally speaking, an animal who weighs less than 4 pounds (1.8 kg) is usually less than desirable as a breeding animal or a show prospect, although there are exceptions to this rule.

There is no typical height for the Chihuahua. The AKC standard clearly states that the dog should be slightly longer than tall. This requirement spans from the very small dog who weighs only 2.5 pounds (1.1 kg) to the dog who weighs nearly the upper limit of 6 pounds (2.7 kg). For this reason, no height can be suggested, since this is a product of the weight of the canine.

Tail

The tail of a typical Chihuahua should be carried up, up and out, or over the back with the tip just touching the back. The tail of

The Chihuahua's skull should appear rounded from ear to ear.

SENIOR DOG TIP

Chihuahua Life Span

Because the Chihuahua is so healthy and long lived, yours may not reach "senior citizen" status until he is in the double digits!

the long-coated Chihuahua is full and very plumy. In the smooth-coated variety, the tail is furry. It does not have a plume like the long coat, but its underside should be nicely coated with visible longer hairs.

Topline

The topline of a typical Chihuahua (the area between the shoulders and the set of the tail) should be flat.

Temperament and Behavioral Traits

The AKC standard describes the Chihuahua as having a "terrier-like" temperament, which explains his feisty personality. These dogs are also totally devoted to their owners and suspicious of strangers. Because they are so tiny, they may find it necessary to assert themselves; after all, the only alternative to making one's presence known and respected is to run and hide—and no self-respecting Chihuahua is going to do that!

Environment

The extremely adaptable Chihuahua is suitable to any environment—urban, suburban, and rural—as long as he is loved and cared for. Obviously, you won't allow your Chihuahua to dodge traffic in the city, wander unattended though a housing development, or go tearing around the countryside by himself, but with you in attendance, your Chihuahua will flourish in any environment.

These dogs are not hardy in very cold weather, so you might want to slip a snazzy sweater

Daily Exercise

Daily exercise is needed for both the physical and mental well-being of your dog. The Chihuahua has different exercise needs than those of larger dogs. In fact, simply retrieving a ball for ten minutes twice a day will probably give the Chihuahua all the exercise he really needs. If you have a fenced yard, your Chihuahua will be able to get enough exercise on his own.

I walk approximately a mile and a half (2.4 km) daily for my own well-being and usually take one of my dogs with me. This walk keeps them in great physical condition, and they enjoy themselves immensely.

onto your pet for twilight strolls in the winter. Small animals generally have less tolerance for the cold than large ones do, and the Chihuahua is probably the least cold-hardy of all the breeds.

Exercise Requirements

One characteristic that endears the Chihuahua to his owner is his exercise requirements. The Chihuahua does not require any rigorous exercise. He can tolerate long walks, but this is not required. The long walk probably does as much or more for the owner than for the dog.

The Chihuahua's

A snazzy sweater or coat will keep your Chihuahua warm on chilly winter walks.

exercise needs are dictated by his size. The larger the Chihuahua, the more exercise he requires. I would venture to say that, given free run of the entire space, most Chihuahuas could live in a small apartment and keep in good condition. However, this breed really enjoys walks with his person. I have a nice, large, fenced backyard, and my dogs run up and down the fenced enclosure when they are allowed the freedom to do so. They love barking at neighborhood cats, children, and other sights and sounds. A fenced yard or a nice large exercise area is required unless the owner is willing to walk a few blocks daily. A Chihuahua who gets no exercise will become a couch potato, which will lead to an obese,

Are Chihuahuas and Kids Compatible?

Chihuahuas make excellent pets for children, as long as the children are gentle, respectful, and properly supervised. Because the Chihuahua is such a tiny dog, there is more danger of a careless or unruly child hurting the dog than vice versa.

she becomes the Chihuahua's teacher. Manipulation is a special gift of the breed. For example, the Chihuahua seems to know that if he doesn't eat what is put in front of him, the person he controls will prepare something special, which most often is less than good for him. Before long, the owner will find herself saying "My dog will eat only rare fillet."

This breed is not unlike an intelligent child who tests limits until she learns that the limits are there to stay. The same is true for the Chihuahua.

Sociability With Other Pets

You must exercise caution when your Chihuahua first meets another canine or feline. His feisty temperament makes for a dog who does not realize that he is small. As far as a Chihuahua is concerned, a Doberman Pinscher should have his space challenged, but too often, the large dog gets the bad press. I would guess most often that the Chihuahua has made the first threat. For this reason, owners need to constantly supervise their pet whenever he is in unfamiliar surroundings (always on a leash).

Although Chihuahuas may not tolerate other dogs well, they are extremely fond of their own breed, which may be

unhealthy pet.

Intelligence

The Chihuahua is an extremely smart dog. He is so intelligent that his owner needs to be sure that

one reason that so many Chihuahua owners have several.

Temperament

The temperament of the Chihuahua per the breed standard is described as "terrier-like." "Terrier-like" in this context means that the Chihuahua has a spicy personality and can be a bit challenging. A shy, quivering pet is not typical of the breed unless he is cold or experiencing sensory overload in a new setting.

Trainability

The Chihuahua is a highly trainable little dog, although every dog is a bit different. Like many small canines with tiny bladders, housetraining can be more of a challenge than with some larger breeds. In addition, because the Chihuahua tends to be territorial, unneutered males may start marking their homes. They do quite well in obedience training and even in agility competition, and a well-socialized Chihuahua makes a superb therapy dog.

The Chihuahua proves that good things come in small packages. Greatness comes from the heart, and no one can doubt the devoted heart of this tiny and noble breed. If you are looking for a dog who has character, charm, and portability rolled neatly into one, look no further.

When properly socialized, most Chihuahuas can learn to get along with other dogs.

Chapter 2

The Stuff of
Everyday
Life

Your new Chihuahua will need a variety of supplies when he comes to live with you. First, a supply of good-quality food and a crate are essential before your puppy arrives home. Once you have purchased a crate and made a food choice, you will need to invest in a variety of secondary items. These include but are not limited to a bed, collar, leash, exercise pen, food and water dishes, gate, grooming supplies, identification, and toys.

Bed

There are many commercially available beds that are appropriate for the Chihuahua. Beds are often chewed, though, so it's important that you keep an eye on your puppy to make sure he's not trying to devour it. The bed that you choose should be a suitable size for the tiny Chihuahua, and it should have a removable cushion or pillow that can be easily laundered.

You can also make a comfy bed for your puppy yourself. A small cardboard box with some foam insulation on the bottom, then covered with a small pillow that has a washable cover, is just as inviting as a purchased item. If you live in a cold climate and decide to use a layer of insulation, be careful that your puppy cannot chew it. The insulation needs to be cut for an exact fit.

Your Chihuahua's bed should be located in a quiet area but still in the vicinity of the family. Chihuahuas like to be near the family but are willing to watch the action from the fringes. Be sure to keep the bed away from drafts that might emanate from air-conditioner vents or poorly sealed entry doors. Also, to keep your Chihuahua warm in winter, you may want to consider elevating the bed slightly off the floor or placing it in an area that receives a few hours of gentle sunlight.

Crate

The use of a crate is crucial for a variety of reasons. For example, the crate can be invaluable if you are having guests over and your puppy is not yet completely socialized. Putting your Chihuahua into a crate can make him feel safe and secure. Also, a puppy can become bored when left alone, but if he is crated, there is no way he can get himself into trouble.

The crate that you choose should be only big enough for your dog to stand up and turn around in easily. Chihuahuas like to relax in a space that fits their

Select a bed that is a suitable size for your tiny dog, and make sure that it has a removable cushion or pillow that can be washed.

body size, because this makes them feel secure. If the crate is too big, your puppy may be tempted to eliminate in one part of it and sleep in another.

Most often, crates are made of plastic, wire, or cloth. Wire crates are fine, but the Chihuahua likes to be warm, so a solid-sided plastic crate might be best. Some Chihuahua owners buy a wire crate and either buy or make a quilt-type covering that can be tied to the wires, which is effective in keeping out drafts. One of the most popular choices for small dogs is a soft-sided crate. These crates are usually made of water-resistant nylon and a steel frame. Most feature a top, front, or side entry, and some come with a reversible fleece/nylon pad and carrying handle. They can fold flat in a matter of seconds. Whatever you choose, make sure that your Chihuahua's crate is made of a washable material.

The bedding in the crate can be anything from an old towel to a specially made mat. These mats are available from the same place that you purchased the crate.

Use the crate consistently in your home, especially when your puppy is very young and not yet trustworthy. It should be a place where your puppy sleeps, especially at night. You also can use the crate to transport your Chihuahua to places like the vet or to confine him when you are traveling away from home.

Setting a Schedule for Your Chihuahua

Dogs adapt to routines, and they like for things to happen on a set schedule. This is why setting a schedule for your Chihuahua is so important. Feeding in the morning one day, at noon the next, and in the evening the following day leads to a confused pet. It also makes housetraining much more difficult. Decide on a routine that fits, and stick with it.

Feeding schedules will change as your dog ages. Puppies need to be fed about three times daily, adolescent puppies can be fed twice daily, and a mature dog should be fed one or two times per day.

Exercise Pen

An exercise pen, often called an x-pen, is essential if your home does not contain a fenced enclosure or you prefer not to allow your dog to run freely around your house or apartment. For the Chihuahua, a minimum of a 2-by 4-foot (0.6- by 1.2-m) exercise pen is needed. These pens almost always fold flat for ease in storage. The pen should be at least 2 feet (0.6 m) tall to assure that your dog stays in the pen. Some Chihuahuas have been known to try to climb out.

Make sure that the pen you select is suitably constructed. Pens that are coated with a vinyl covering over the metal are best because they do not rust. I have known of pet owners who have purchased a baby playpen at a yard sale. These are usually available for a reasonable price and can serve the purpose of an x-pen quite nicely as long as they are thoroughly cleaned after each use.

Your pet's safety should be a primary concern. Setting up the exercise pen where your Chihuahua can enjoy the outdoors without being in hot sun in the summer is an important consideration.

Food and Water

A Chihuahua eats very little, so you should buy the best food that you can afford. It is critical that your puppy learn to eat this food rather than special treats. Water should be available at all times, and the water dish should always be in the same spot. Place the water dish in a spot where it won't be accidentally knocked over.

Food and Water Dishes

There are three main types of bowls that are commercially available: stainless steel, plastic, and ceramic, with stainless steel being the best choice. These bowls are a

The crate that you choose for your dog should be large enough for him to stand up and turn around in easily.

bit more expensive, but they will last a lifetime, and they are easily sanitized in the dishwasher. Plastic dishes are not suitable for dogs, as a dog can develop a skin allergy from them; in fact, most cases of chin dermatitis are simply the result of eating from plastic dishes. Ceramic bowls are sturdy and pretty, but they can break or develop tiny fissures in which bacteria thrive. Stick with stainless steel, and purchase the smallest bowl available for your tiny Chihuahua.

Collar

Generally, collars that are designed for cats are better choices for a Chihuahua than dog collars are. Cat collars are usually made of a pliable material, like nylon, that is gentler on the dog than a firm, rigid leather collar would be. Choke collars and other collars made

The Expert Knows

Dogs and the Law

People are responsible for learning the rules and laws that govern where they live when it comes to their pets. For example, some locales require all pets to be neutered or have rabies shots. The only way to learn of these limits is to inquire. Animal shelters, animal control officers, and veterinarians are all good sources to ask.

for obedience training are poorly suited for this tiny breed, because a sharp tug could result in a collapsed trachea. In fact, a harness is a safer option, especially for puppies, than a collar is. The harness should fit snugly but not tightly. Cat harnesses are a good choice because they are lightweight and pliable.

Purchasing the correct-size collar for your puppy is important, and you will need to purchase two or maybe three collars as he grows. A collar that fits properly should be snug enough so that the head cannot slip through yet loose enough for a finger to be inserted under the collar easily. As your puppy grows, you will need to monitor the tightness of the collar.

When you can no longer easily get a finger under the collar, it is time to get a larger one.

Leash

The leash is an important purchase for your Chihuahua. The one that you choose should be made of a lightweight material, such as durable, machine-washable nylon. A good leash is 4 to 6 feet (1.2 to 1.8 m) long and narrow enough so that it looks like it belongs to a Chihuahua and not a Rottweiler. If you can't resist the idea of a rhinestone-studded leash, go right ahead. Your dog deserves it.

The leash should be kept away from the puppy except when in use. This is because the leash, like a food or water dish, can be perceived as a toy or something to chew on, depending on the material. The danger of choking on swallowed parts of a leash, and the destruction of the leash itself, are both good reasons to keep it safely away from the puppy.

Puppies who are accustomed to walks on a leash will soon learn that they can anticipate a fun activity with their owner. A leash can also be used for housetraining outside. Dogs should never be allowed to roam without a leash until basic obedience behaviors are learned.

Gate

You will need a gate to keep your Chihuahua in safe areas inside your

Dog Sitters

Dog sitters are available to care for your pet when you're not around. A pet sitter will actually come to your home, not just to walk your pet but to feed, care for, or even medicate him if needed. A good pet sitter is bonded and insured, and she can provide references. She is courteous and professional and ideally will be a member of Pet Sitters International or a similar organization. A good pet sitter will visit your home before her assignment actually starts to meet your dog and get detailed information about his care. At this time, she should provide a written document stating both her services and fees. Make sure that any potential dog sitter responds well to your Chihuahua.

home. Two gates might be necessary if you have an inquisitive pet who likes to wander everywhere. For example, you may decide to place a gate at the entrance to the bathroom and at the head of a stairway.

When selecting a gate, you need only to know the width of the opening where you are going to use it. Once you know this, determine if hardware is required. Some gates, known as tension-mounted gates, require no hardware. Check to be sure that the gate you are considering has bars spaced closely enough to prevent your Chihuahua from slipping through. Gates used for infants are often suitable for the Chihuahua.

If you want your dog to have full run of the house once he is housetrained, the

investment in a gate may not be necessary. Creative barriers can be made from cardboard boxes, expandable window screens, and other household items. Chihuahuas can negotiate stairs with no challenge once they have grown a bit and know the location of the stairs.

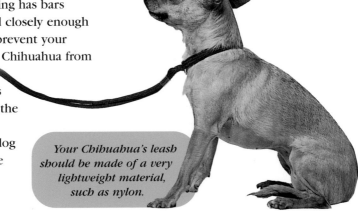

Your Chihuahua's leash should be made of a very lightweight material, such as nylon.

Grooming Supplies
The Chihuahua is often referred to as a wash-and-wear breed. This simply

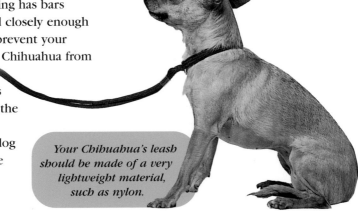

FAMILY-FRIENDLY TIP

Children as Caregivers

If you are the parent of a child, buying a puppy and expecting your child to be his primary caregiver is bound to fail, even if the child is an adolescent. An adult needs to be willing to be the primary caregiver. The child can be taught to assist with care, but no child should be expected to shoulder total responsibility. Such a situation can lead only to frustration on the part of the child, who may grow to resent the pet, and the dog will most likely be the one to suffer.

For more detailed grooming information, please see Chapter 4.

Identification

Even the most careful pet owner can accidentally lose her pet if he escapes the house or yard. This is a terribly frightening experience for a pet owner. However, the trauma can be somewhat minimized if the dog has identification.

One popular identification option is the dog tag. These tags have the owner's name, address, and telephone number permanently stamped onto or into a metal tag. This method of identification is widely available.

A much better permanent

means that he has little need for grooming. The smooth variety has fewer grooming needs than the long-coated variety.

The grooming tools you need are basic. They include a comb with fine teeth (a stainless steel comb is recommended), a slicker brush, a pin brush, a pair of scissors with blunt ends, and a hair dryer. (Most households have more than one hair dryer, and a different one for the pet is not required.) If you own a smooth-coated Chihuahua, the pin brush is probably not needed.

identification method is the microchip, in addition to dog tags. A veterinarian usually offers this service, which is a nearly painless process in which a microchip with a unique number is inserted just under the skin at the shoulders. If your dog becomes lost, an animal shelter or veterinarian can scan the dog for this chip. Once the microchip number is determined, the registry with which the number is registered can help the shelter learn the identity of the pet's owner.

Toys

The selection of appropriately sized toys is critical to your Chihuahua's safety. In fact, you should buy only toys that your dog cannot put fully into his mouth. Also, pay careful attention to small parts that could be chewed off and swallowed.

Some toys are what are commonly called "chew toys" and can be a great solution to having inappropriate items gnawed, especially during the teething stage.

Some toys designed for cats are ideal for Chihuahua puppies. Cat balls are often smaller than dog balls, but care needs to be exercised with balls that have bells in them. These bells have been known to come out or be chewed out, and what was designed as a playful noisemaker could be lethal if swallowed. Puppies even like catnip toys, but the toy should be monitored and discarded before its contents are ready to fall out.

SENIOR DOG TIP

Helping Your Older Dog Adjust

If you have adopted an older Chihuahua, expect him to be a bit more reserved initially than a younger dog might be. He may have bonded with a former owner and need some time to adjust. Sitting quietly and stroking your older dog while talking softly to him is usually soothing and will help him relax. Your senior Chihuahua will usually make the transition to his new home in two weeks' time.

Because they are so intelligent, Chihuahuas are quick to learn to fetch. This activity with a favorite toy will give both you and your puppy many minutes or even hours of fun. This is also a great bonding activity.

Your Chihuahua doesn't ask for much in life other than your undying love, great food, a comfortable bed, sufficient exercise, proper neckwear, and dashing food and water bowls. It's part of the fun of dog ownership to provide him with this stuff of everyday life!

The Stuff of Everyday Life

Chapter 3

Good Eating

Your Chihuahua cannot find his own food, and he doesn't know what is healthiest for him. For these reasons, selecting a quality food and knowing how much to feed is critical for aiding a young puppy's growth, maintaining an adult dog's condition, and keeping an aging pet as healthy as possible.

Serving your dog a quality diet is similar to serving your favorite wine or cut of meat—it will most likely cost a few cents more. Chihuahuas eat very little, so it's important that the food you choose be the best that you can provide. This chapter will provide you with the tools you need to make an informed decision regarding your dog's diet.

Nutrients

While dogs are classed as carnivores on the basis of their dentition, they are functional omnivores—meaning they enjoy and can thrive on a wide variety of foods. Like humans, dogs need the basic building blocks of nutrition. These include proteins, fats, carbohydrates, vitamins, minerals, and water. A proper blend of nutrients is essential for good muscle tone, strong bones, and healthy skin.

Proteins

More important than the total amount of protein is its quality. Dogs do best on meat- or fish-derived proteins; vegetable-derived proteins are more difficult to digest and can cause diarrhea. Dogs thrive on meat—not corn, soybeans, rice, or wheat. In general, a dog's diet should be about 75 percent meat and the rest vegetables.

Puppies and senior dogs require a higher protein diet than do young adults. Some high-protein commercial

The proper balance of fats is critical for a healthy coat and skin.

diets are made especially for active working or hunting dogs. Since your Chihuahua is neither, a high-protein diet is not necessary.

Fats

Fats are necessary components of your Chihuahua's diet. They not only increase the palatability of food, but they also allow fat-soluble vitamins to be absorbed into the body. They are also critical for a healthy coat and skin, reproductive efficiency, and kidney function. Dogs can use plant and animal fats with equal ease.

Most commercial dry dog foods contain between 5 and 10 percent fat, a sufficient amount for sedentary dogs. Too much fat, however, especially when given all at once, can result in pancreatic problems and obesity.

Carbohydrates

Carbohydrates are not essential to the canine diet, because dogs can make them themselves from fat and protein. However, carbohydrates are a cheap and easy form of energy—as long as they don't make up too much of a dog's diet.

Vitamins

Vitamins are plant- and animal-derived substances necessary for your dog's health. They are naturally present only in tiny amounts, but they are essential for life.

Vitamins are divided into water-soluble and fat-soluble types. Water-soluble vitamins include the B-complex vitamins and vitamin C. The B vitamins help convert food to energy. Dogs can manufacture their own vitamin C, so supplementation is not usually necessary. However, dogs under stress may benefit from a little extra; it certainly won't hurt them.

Fat-soluble vitamins are A, D, E, and K. Stored in the body, these vitamins are the ones in danger of being oversupplemented.

Minerals

Defined as any inorganic component of a food, minerals are essential for bone development, muscle function, fluid balance, and nervous system function. Just like people, dogs need the following minerals in their diets: calcium, phosphorus, potassium, salt, magnesium, iron, copper, manganese, zinc, iodine, and selenium. Zinc is especially important, as it is needed to regulate metabolism. A diet deficient in zinc will result in thin hair and crusty dermatitis.

Water

Always provide your Chihuahua with plenty of fresh, clean water to drink. Dogs need between ½ to ¾ fluid ounce (14.8 to 22.2 ml) of water per 1 pound (0.45 kg) of body weight per

day. This includes the water taken in through food. You don't need to calculate this; just keep plenty of fresh water available all the time.

Understanding Food Labels

Understanding a dog food label can be difficult, but the careful consumer can figure out at least some of it. It may come as a surprise to learn that as far as federal regulations go, very little is actually required of pet food manufacturers. Companies are required to accurately identify the product, provide the net quantity, give their

Always provide your Chihuahua with plenty of fresh, clean drinking water

Novelty Kibble

Although some dog food manufacturers attempt to make their dog food appear palatable by giving it a novelty shape or attractive color, dogs don't care at all if their food looks appealing. Tiny pieces shaped like bones, for example, are no more readily eaten than normally shaped kibble. The presence of quality ingredients is much more important than a food's appearance.

address, and correctly list ingredients. However, pet food companies are not subject to quality-control laws. A little security is found by looking for the Association of American Feed Control Officials (AAFCO) label. This organization provides model regulations that pet foods must follow in order to carry the AAFCO label.

AAFCO-labeled foods provide a guaranteed analysis of the food, a calorie statement, and a nutritional adequacy statement. This doesn't necessarily mean that the product is good—it just means that it's properly labeled. Critics claim that the testing AAFCO performs is not particularly stringent and is in no way tantamount to a controlled scientific study. However, the good news is that the highly competitive dog food market is driving up the overall quality of commercial foods. Today, owners have more good choices than ever before; however, they also need to educate themselves to know what they're buying.

"Meat" Labels

If an AAFCO-labeled product has the word *beef* in its name, it must be 95 percent beef exclusive of water needed for processing. Even counting the water, it must be 70 percent beef. These products are all canned and have simple names, like "Jean's Beef Food for Dogs." The same goes for chicken, fish, and lamb.

"Dinner" Labels

If the word *dinner*, or a similar word like *platter* or *entrée* is used, each featured ingredient must compose between 25 and 94 percent of the total. Therefore, "Richard's Beef Dinner for Dogs" must contain at least 25 percent beef.

When deciding on a commercial diet, choose a food with high-quality ingredients.

"With" Labels

If the word *with* is used, the named ingredient must be at least 3 percent of the total. Thus, "Diane's Sawdust Dinner for Dogs With Liver" must contain 3 percent liver. "Diane's Beef Dinner for Dogs With Chicken and Fish" must contain 3 percent chicken and 3 percent fish, as well as at least 25 percent beef.

"Flavor" Labels

If the label reads "Beef Flavor" rather than "Beef," it need only contain enough beef to be detectable. The word *flavor* must appear in letters as large as those of the named ingredient.

Commercial Diets

Commercial dog foods come in a variety of shapes, sizes, and textures. Three basic types are available: dry, semi-moist, and canned.

Dry Food (Kibble)

Kibble is a convenient, nutritionally adequate food for dogs. Dry food helps reduce tartar buildup on teeth, but not as much as brushing the teeth does. And it doesn't do anything for cleaning the canine teeth (the fangs), since chewing is done with the back teeth. In comparison with other food choices, dry food is the least expensive, largely because of its high grain content. It also tends to be low in fat.

Some people like to feed their dogs a basic diet of kibble, with different added foods every day, such as green beans, carrots, gravy, or canned meat. This plan gives your dog adequate nutrition and variety.

Keep Kibble Fresh

Keep in mind that improperly stored food can become loaded with molds and other deadly toxins. To reduce the chances of your dog getting sick from these things, be sure to use the freshest foods available, and keep the food bag tightly closed. Also, try not to buy kibble in bulk—smaller bags get used more quickly and stay fresher longer. Always remove and discard your dog's uneaten portion of dry food after approximately 20 minutes to prevent spoilage.

Choose a Food With Quality Ingredients

When deciding on a commercial diet, choose a food that has the specific name of a meat (beef, chicken, turkey) listed as the first ingredient. Foods that just say "meat" or "poultry" should be avoided. Unfortunately, just because a product has meat or poultry as the first

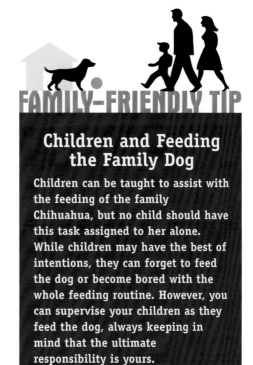

FAMILY-FRIENDLY TIP

Children and Feeding the Family Dog

Children can be taught to assist with the feeding of the family Chihuahua, but no child should have this task assigned to her alone. While children may have the best of intentions, they can forget to feed the dog or become bored with the whole feeding routine. However, you can supervise your children as they feed the dog, always keeping in mind that the ultimate responsibility is yours.

ingredient doesn't mean that the product is mostly meat or poultry.

Good food should not contain sweeteners, artificial flavors, artificial colors, or artificial preservatives. The best dog foods are preserved naturally with vitamin E (tocopherols) or vitamin C.

Avoid dog food containing "by-products." Meat by-products are the part of the animal not deemed fit for human consumption, and while a few by-products are healthy and tasty to dogs, many more are not. And since the label doesn't tell you exactly what the by-products are, you're better off not getting foods that contain them.

Semi-Moist Food

Semi-moist food is about 25 percent water and can be just as high in sugar, in the form of corn syrup, beet pulp, sucrose, and caramel. Your dog does not need this stuff, which promotes obesity and tooth decay. The shelf life of these products is also lower than that of either canned or dry food.

Semi-moist foods usually are packaged in cellophane. Once opened, any food that is left over needs to be placed in a tight container to keep it from drying out and attracting insects. Semi-moist foods that are not consumed by your pet once they are opened may or may not need to be refrigerated. The product label should clearly tell you of the need to refrigerate once the food is opened. To prevent it from spoiling, withdraw your Chihuahua's uneaten semi-moist food after about 20 minutes.

Canned Food

I have fed my Chihuahuas many varieties of canned foods, which they enjoy immensely. In fact, given the choice, most dogs would probably choose to eat canned foods over dry or semi-moist foods—just the aroma of the food is extremely appetizing to a dog.

Canned food is much more

Consult your veterinarian if you decide to feed your Chihuahua a noncommercial diet.

expensive than kibble, even though it is about 75 percent water. It can be useful for mixing with dry food, however, since most dogs find canned food to be highly palatable. Dogs who have urinary tract infections often thrive better on canned dog foods than on kibble, mostly because of the increased water in canned foods.

A Chihuahua can get about three meals out of one can of food. Leftover food should be stored in the refrigerator, although this can be a problem because most dogs don't like cold food. If you have time to heat up your Chihuahua's food prior to serving it, though, that will solve the problem. Always withdraw canned food after about 20 minutes, just as you would for dry and semi-moist foods.

Some dogs do not tolerate canned food as well as semi-moist or dry. One way you will be able to determine whether your Chihuahua is unable to tolerate canned food is through his stool. A dog's stool should be firm and well shaped when his food passes through the digestive tract. A loose stool indicates that the food may not agree with him. If you have just changed your dog's food to canned, you can expect the stool to change. However, if the stool does not return to a firm, well-shaped appearance, canned food is probably not a good choice for your dog. Dogs are much like humans; what one dog can eat, another cannot.

SENIOR DOG TIP

Feeding the Senior Dog

Older dogs have special dietary requirements, especially a need for more protein (unless they have kidney trouble), than young adults require. They also benefit from arginine (an essential amino acid that stimulates the immune system), omega-3 fatty acids (to keep their brain and nervous system in good repair), and less phosphorus (to maintain general health). You should consider feeding a commercial food that is specially processed for the aging pet. Consult your veterinarian for advice on what to feed your senior Chihuahua.

Similar to older humans, older animals tend to have a slower metabolism and require fewer calories to maintain their weight, so keep an eye on your senior Chihuahua's waistline. Also, like many small dogs, the Chihuahua seems to be predisposed to losing his teeth earlier than some larger breeds. For this reason, it is essential to know when or if an alternative food texture might be necessary for your aging dog. Simply dampening a dry food, for example, may become necessary as your Chihuahua ages.

Good Eating

Noncommercial Diets

A noncommercial diet, which can be either home cooked or raw, is a fancy way of saying "do it yourself." If you'd like to feed your dog a raw or home-cooked diet, your best option is to consult with a veterinary nutritionist about how to make sure that it is nutritionally balanced and complete.

Home-Cooked Foods

While cooking your dog's food at home isn't as easy as opening a bag of kibble, it's not really much harder, either. However, preparing a diet at home does require some training. The main dangers from such diets are a calcium/phosphorus imbalance, as well as inadequate levels of calcium, copper, iodine, and certain vitamins, especially the fat-soluble ones and some B vitamins.

Home-cooked diets are often chosen to resolve the picky-eater syndrome. As mentioned in Chapter 1, the Chihuahua is a master of manipulation. If he learns that refusing to eat a dry food diet will lead to a home-cooked meal, he will make the obvious choice. Commercial dog foods are

the result of years of research, and some don't feel that most home-cooked diets can be totally nutritionally correct for the Chihuahua.

Raw Diets

One of the major trends in dog nutrition today is the raw diet, which often includes raw bones. Proponents of the diet claim that dogs in the wild consumed raw food and thrived on it. Those who are against the raw diet claim that raw meat may contain bacteria and worms, making it an unsafe choice for today's domesticated dogs. Be

If you want a fit dog, feed him the proper amount at scheduled times.

sure to consult your veterinarian before deciding on the raw diet.

Supplements

Supplements are any nutrients that are added to a dog's diet. They can include vitamins, minerals, or herbs. You may be tempted from time to time to add a particular supplement to your Chihuahua's food. However, if you buy a quality food, additives are not required. In fact, adding extra vitamins without consulting your vet can even be harmful to your dog.

The skin and coat of a Chihuahua is a good indicator of his general well-being. The coat should be shiny, and his skin should be soft and pliable. There should not be an accumulation of dander on the skin. The coat should be inviting to stroke, without a dead-straw feel.

Treats

Dogs love treats, and the Chihuahua is no exception. However, the use of treats requires discipline on your part, because too many can lead to a spoiled, overweight pet.

Treats should reinforce a desired behavior. For example, reward your dog for eliminating in the proper spot or for performing an obedience command correctly, like *sit* or *down*. Basically, your Chihuahua should earn his treat. Be sure that you don't reward your dog if he has not done what you want, as this can reinforce an unacceptable behavior.

There are a variety of treats

Table Manners

Promoting good table manners in your Chihuahua will make for much more pleasant meals for you and your family. To encourage good manners, never feed your dog from the table. Try giving him his meal at the same time that you sit down to eat. If you decide you want to feed him a treat from the table, go into a different room and offer him the tidbit there so that he doesn't associate it with the table and consequently learn to beg. A begging dog is a real turnoff for guests, and caving in to your dog's demand for table food may lead to an overweight dog who no longer eats his regular food.

available commercially for pets. If you go into the pet food aisle of your local grocery or discount store, you will be able to find a wide variety of commercially prepared treats, such as bones, biscuits, and liver morsels. You can also serve your Chihuahua homemade treats, such as liver cookies, for example. Small pieces of carrot or morsels of hot dog also work well.

Making sure that your dog receives enough exercise will help prevent obesity.

Keep in mind that for a Chihuahua, the smaller the treat, the better; a pea-sized treat is fine for most purposes. The other critical consideration is that your Chihuahua should learn that treats reward good behavior—they are not the main course.

Feeding Schedules

Mammals are programmed to be hungry all the time, and if they had their choice, they would like to be eating all the time. Letting a dog act on these desires is called "free feeding." This method entails just filling up the food bowl in the morning and continuing to fill it up all day. Scheduled feeding, as opposed to free feeding, involves a sense of timing. You decide how many times and when you are going to feed your dog, and you give him food at those times.

Free Feeding

It's hard to monitor how much a free-fed dog is actually consuming, and if you own more than one dog, you won't know who's getting the food. There are a variety of other disadvantages to free feeding your Chihuahua as well. For one, leaving food out all day for your dog may attract insects. Also, dogs who are allowed to free feed are usually obese as a result. In the past, dogs in the wild were programmed to gorge themselves because they didn't know when they would have another meal. Domestic dogs don't really have this worry anymore, but they will still try to eat as much as they can as often as they can, which results in an overweight pet. In addition, free-fed dogs are much harder to housetrain, because they will need to eliminate at unpredictable times throughout the day.

Scheduled Feeding

If you want a fit dog, feed him a proper amount at scheduled times; don't let him decide for himself. Dogs don't make good decisions about these things. The genetic heritage of dogs encourages them to gorge when food is available, and even though your Chihuahua hasn't been out hunting caribou in a long, long time, his genes don't know that. Where food is concerned, he still thinks that he's a wolf.

In most cases, scheduled feeding is the best of all worlds. You will be able to determine how much your dog eats and when, which will help you to control his weight. In addition, he will be

While some dogs don't mind sharing a food dish, sharing meals can lead to fights and competitive eating.

Foods to Avoid

The following foods can be toxic to dogs and should be avoided:

- **Grapes and raisins:** Grapes and raisins can cause acute kidney failure in dogs, although the reason is not known.
- **Chocolate:** Chocolate, and baker's chocolate especially, can cause a range of problems, including cardiovascular difficulties and seizures.
- **Onions:** Onions can induce hemolytic anemia.

easier to housetrain, because he will be eliminating more regularly than if he was fed at random times throughout the day.

To make scheduled feeding work for you and your Chihuahua, be aware of how much food your dog will consume in a 20-minute interval. If he doesn't eat all his food within this timeframe, take it away. He will soon learn that he has to eat within those 20 minutes or wait until the next meal.

Obesity

Canine obesity is the result of too much food and not enough activity.

Contrary to popular belief, obesity does not result from neutering your pet. It can, however, be directly traced to an owner who has not fed her dog on a schedule or who has neglected to provide her dog with a sufficient amount of exercise.

The average Chihuahua can weigh anywhere from 3 to 6 pounds (1.4 to 2.7 kg), and it is fairly simple to determine whether or not he is obese. A Chihuahua in good condition should have a spine and ribs that can be felt easily under a thin layer of fatty tissue. If you have to probe to feel either the spine or the ribs, you have an obese dog.

Dogs are usually obese simply because they consume too many calories or lack adequate exercise. The first thing to do with an obese pet, then, is to limit his food intake and increase his exercise. Be cautious, though; a brisk walk around a block or two may be all your obese Chihuahua can tolerate. Heavy panting and lying down are indicators that your dog is exhausted and that you should end the exercise session. If after six weeks of food limitation and exercise your pet is not showing evidence of weight loss, it is time to consult your veterinarian.

I used to dog-sit an obese Chihuahua for a couple who spent the winter in a warmer setting. I was given instructions on what to feed her—mostly low-quality foods that

A Chihuahua in good condition should have a spine and ribs that can be felt easily.

were unhealthy and made her gain even more weight. Interestingly enough, when I fed the dog healthy foods that her owners had said she wouldn't eat at home, she ate them gladly. When the couple returned to get their dog, they said in surprise, "I don't know what you do, but she won't eat like this for us at home." The answer is that the dog had learned to manipulate her owners, knowing that they would not require her to eat a healthy diet. If the owners had made her eat what was good for her, though, she would not have become overweight. This story serves as a reminder that if your pet is obese, you

should look no further than the reflection in the mirror—it is up to you to help your Chihuahua get back on the road to health.

Eating well for a human adult does not usually include desserts at every meal and a bowl of ice cream before bed. While this may be appealing, we know that our bodies take a beating when we indulge. The same is true for your pet; feeding him an unhealthy diet will lead to obesity and a variety of other health problems. Feeding him a healthy, nutritious diet, on the other hand, will give him energy and help him to live a longer life.

Chapter 4

Looking Good

Good grooming makes your dog look and feel like the special pet he is. In fact, a well-groomed Chihuahua will look more beautiful, feel healthier, and be more confident in your affection. That's a pretty impressive list of benefits for just a few minutes of your time every week!

The time to begin grooming your new Chihuahua is day one in his new home. Don't wait to begin until shedding is out of control or mats have formed behind your pet's ears. If you make grooming a daily routine, it should take no more than five to ten minutes.

Coat and Skin Care

A healthy coat and skin are products of good nutrition more so than they are of brushing and bathing. In fact, too much bathing can lead to dry and flaky skin. However, your Chihuahua does need to be brushed and bathed—the appropriate question is, how much and how often should you do so?

Brushing

Let's begin our discussion with brushing. Daily brushing is essential for both smooth- and long-coated Chihuahuas. The brush type varies between coats, but gently brushing down to the skin is essential for both coats. In fact, brushing both coat types from tail to head (against the growth pattern of the coat) is essential to remove the dead coat and keep shedding to a minimum.

For a smooth-coated Chihuahua, a slicker brush, which is designed to untangle hair and prevent mats, can work if you are careful not to brush too aggressively. A smooth-coated Chihuahua's coat will not mat, but it will shed year-round. A better option

Grooming Supplies

1. brush (slicker for smooth and long coats, soft bristle for smooth coats, or pin for long coats)
2. cotton balls
3. dog toothbrush and toothpaste
4. hair dryer
5. metal comb
6. mild shampoo and cream rinse
7. nail clipper and file
8. towels

might be a soft bristle brush with natural bristles. These brushes are more expensive than other types, because they are especially gentle, but they are well worth the difference in price.

A long-coated Chihuahua can be brushed with a slicker brush or pin brush, which lifts out loose hair and debris in long-coated dogs. A comb with wide teeth can also work well. Long-coated Chihuahuas will mat, especially behind the ears and around the anus. If a mat does occur, care needs to be exercised regarding its removal. The easiest way to remove the mat is to make several cuts with the direction of the hair, not across the hair. Gentle brushing will then allow the mat to be removed. Long-coated Chihuahuas also tend to shed more seasonally. Bitches (females) who are not spayed will shed profusely after each estral period, which is a good reason to have your Chihuahua spayed.

Your Chihuahua's slicker, pin, or bristle brushes should be kept clean of hair, which you can easily accomplish using a metal comb. Use either the fine or coarse end of the comb to rid the brush of accumulated hair. (The spacing of the bristles in your brush will determine which end of the comb to use.) Dogs who are kept clean will not require their brushes to be washed on a regular schedule. I don't recommend washing your slicker brush, because it is constructed of metal bristles and can rust. If you do decide to rinse the brush, dry it carefully either in direct sunlight or with a hair dryer. A rusted brush can result in its teeth breaking off or the discoloration of your Chihuahua's coat.

How to Brush Your Chihuahua

Begin with your Chihuahua positioned either on a grooming table or on a large bath towel situated on your lap. Whichever you choose, your dog needs to be taught to accept being positioned on his back for part of the process.

When brushing your Chihuahua, begin at the base of the tail and brush

A wide-toothed comb will lift out loose hair and debris in the long-coated Chihuahua.

The Expert Knows

Grooming as a Health Check

While grooming your Chihuahua, use the time to evaluate the overall health of your pet. Check his eyes—are they tearing? Check his weight—can you easily find his ribs and backbone? Smell his ears—is there a foul smell present? Check his skin—is it dry or flaky? You should also check for fleas and ticks, and if you find any, eliminate them immediately.

you have finished brushing your Chihuahua in this manner, you are ready to smooth the coat back into its normal pattern. This entire process should take no more than five minutes if done on a regular basis.

Keep in mind that brushing should be done down to the skin; just brushing the surface of the coat will do no good. Also, you may want to try talking softly to your dog in a reassuring tone of voice, as this will help him to relax.

Keep an eye out for small black specks at the base of the tail and elsewhere in the coat, which may indicate a flea infestation. If you find specks, gather them and place them on a damp paper towel. If the moisture causes them to dissolve into red spots on the paper towel, your dog has fleas. These black specks are actually flea feces that contain your dog's digested blood.

Bathing

Chihuahuas who are brushed often need only be bathed once a month or every six weeks. Choose a shampoo that is gentle and formulated especially for dogs. You will also need a good cream rinse made for dogs.

How to Bathe Your Chihuahua

When getting ready to bathe your Chihuahua, first decide whether you are going to wash him in the bathtub or in

against the grain of the coat toward the head. If you find any mats, carefully cut through them with scissors. (As mentioned earlier, to get rid of a mat, make a couple of cuts parallel to the hair shafts—not across them. After making these cuts, you can easily brush the mat away.) Next, brush the legs, beginning with the feet and then moving upward toward the body. Be careful when brushing the armpit area of the front legs, because this is a mat-prone area. Don't forget to brush the area under the tail, down the back of the hind legs, and under the chin. Both males and females should have the hair around their genitals trimmed so that they do not urinate on their coat. Once the sink—and then be sure to bathe him in the same place in the future. Using the bathtub one time and the sink the next will only confuse your pet and possibly make him anxious.

Use a soothing tone of voice when introducing your puppy to the area in which he will eventually receive his bath. Don't run the water until you can feel him relax. Once he appears calm, run the water, making sure that it is on the cool side of warm. Thoroughly wet your dog before you add shampoo. (I recommend a shampoo that will cause no irritation to the dog's eyes, because tear staining is such a problem in many Chihuahuas that you will need to thoroughly wash the area around the eyes.) Apply the shampoo from the head to the base of the tail. Gently massage the shampoo into the coat down to the skin. Apply the same massaging action to the legs, under the chin, and on the underbelly. Be sure to wash the feet. When you are finished shampooing, rinse your Chihuahua, and then shampoo him again. Rinse him thoroughly.

Next, apply a fresh-smelling conditioner and work it into the coat. I often even take a wide-toothed comb and comb the conditioner into the coat. Once you have done this, rinse your pet thoroughly. Thorough rinsing is critically important, and failure to do so

properly can result in skin irritation.

Once you have finished bathing and rinsing your dog, you will need to towel-dry him to soak up the excess water. Next, use a hair dryer to get him completely dry. Make sure that it is not set on a hot heat setting, and be careful not to hold the dryer too close to him, or you may burn him. Chihuahuas hate to be cold, so thorough drying is necessary. The end product should be a sparkling-clean coat that actually does sparkle in direct sunlight.

Nail Care

Your Chihuahua's nails should be kept short, so if you can hear them clicking when he walks on tile, linoleum, or wood floors, it is time for a trim.

Nail trimming is important for a variety of reasons. Long nails can snag

Daily brushing is essential for both smooth- and long-coated Chihuahuas.

Trimming the Feet

Long-coated Chihuahuas will require the hair on their feet to be trimmed for neatness and to keep them from tracking debris into the house. This process is easily accomplished with a blunt pair of scissors. Trim around the perimeter of the foot and between the pads. If you begin to trim your Chihuahua's feet from the time he first comes to live with you, he won't find it stressful.

clothing, carpeting, and upholstery. They can also cause painful scratches. Nails can even become so long that they begin to curl and grow into the pads of the foot, a serious problem that will affect your Chihuahua's gait and cause him a great deal of pain.

Chihuahuas who rarely walk on uncarpeted surfaces may have nails that are unacceptably long. One way to prevent your dog's nails from reaching unacceptable lengths is to make sure that you trim them every time you give him a bath.

Nail trimming requires nail clippers, a cauterizing powder in case you cut too far, and perhaps a file. (A human toenail clipper is acceptable, although clippers that are specifically designed for canine nails are readily available.)

How to Trim Your Chihuahua's Nails

Ideally, you should begin trimming (or pretending to trim) your dog's feet from the time he is a youngster. Constantly playing with his feet will get him accustomed to the idea—you absolutely can't start this too early!

To trim your Chihuahua's nails, take his paw gently in your hand, and softly squeeze it to extend the nails. Clip the tip quickly, and be careful to avoid the quick—the blood vessel that runs nearly to the end of the nail. You can't see it in dark-nailed dogs, so you'll need to clip just a tiny bit at a time. However, if you look closely, you'll notice a small white spot at the tip of the nail as the clip approaches the vein. Stop there—this is the quick.

If you cut into the quick, your dog's nail will bleed, which is painful for him. The bleeding can be quickly stopped with a cauterizing agent, such as styptic powder. If your dog's nails have some ragged edges after you've clipped them, smooth them with a nail file.

Ear Care

A Chihuahua with healthy ears will not paw at them, and they will not

The Grooming Table

Any surface can be used as a grooming site for your Chihuahua, as long as it is steady and contains a nonslip surface. Special grooming tables are available for purchase as well. I use a small plywood board that has legs approximately 1 inch (2.5 cm) high. The board is covered with rubber matting and is surrounded with a wooden edging. There are a variety of tables available, including types with folding chrome legs and others with an arm that features a noose to hold the dog's head steady. You have to decide what works best for you. Choose whatever option appeals to you, always keeping your dog's safety and comfort in mind.

emit a foul odor. If your Chihuahua does paw at his ears, he may have ear mites. Ear mites live in the debris of the ear, and the crawling sensation of the mites creates an itch that needs to be scratched. You will need to take your pet to the vet if he paws at his ears excessively or if you otherwise suspect that he is suffering from an ear infection.

Fortunately, one virtually foolproof safeguard against ear mites and infection is a healthy, clean ear, which you can foster with regular examinations and cleanings.

How to Clean Your Chihuahua's Ears

Make ear cleaning part of your bath-time routine. To clean the ear, moisten a cotton ball with alcohol, and gently wipe the inner flap of the ear, including the crevices. Be sure not to stick the cotton ball down into the ear. If you find that the ear is oozing, moist, or smelly, take your Chihuahua to the veterinarian. A healthy canine ear will have no odor, and it won't emit any discharge. In a healthy Chihuahua, the ear leather should appear relatively clean. Because the Chihuahua has an erect ear, he is less likely to have ear problems than breeds with floppy ears.

Eye Care

The Chihuahua should have a very full—but not protruding—eye. These

Keep your Chihuahua's nails short with regular trimming.

Looking Good

full eyes make the Chihuahua a common target for problems. The hair around a healthy eye should not be tear stained. If it is, consult with your veterinarian to find out what is causing the staining.

Take care when bathing your Chihuahua that no shampoo enters his eye. A gentle dog shampoo that does not cause eye irritation is best.

How to Clean Your Chihuahua's Eye Area

To clean your Chihuahua's eye area, take a dampened cloth or tissue and gently wipe around the eye. Pay particular attention to the inner corners of the eyes. Cleaning this area every few days is a small time commitment, but it will help to ward off potential problems.

Grooming as Bonding Time

Grooming time is an excellent opportunity to bond with your pet. For this reason, don't begin to groom him when you are overly tired or stressed. During grooming sessions, speak softly to your dog in a soothing, reassuring manner. This will help him relax and learn to enjoy this special time that you have together.

To clean your dog's eye area, take a dampened cloth or tissue and gently wipe around the eye.

Dental Care

Chihuahuas are especially prone to dental problems. One reason is simply that they are small dogs, and small dogs have a crowded jaw.

Dental disease can be deadly serious in dogs—it's not just about bad breath. In fact, along with obesity, dental disease is probably one of the leading causes of death in dogs. The buildup of bacteria under the gum line can get into the bloodstream and damage the kidneys and heart valves.

Good dental care means brushing your Chihuahua's teeth *every day*. I know that this can be an inconvenience, and you might not be able to keep to such a strict schedule, but the more often you brush your dog's teeth, the better his dental health will be. If you don't brush your dog's teeth every day, do so as often as you can.

Begin brushing your Chihuahua's teeth from the time he is a puppy; 8 to 12 weeks old is not too early. Your puppy may not look as if he needs his teeth brushed, but getting him used to the process early on will make things easier later. Don't wait until your dog is actually showing signs of dental disease—by this time, it's too late.

When you brush his teeth, inspect the gums. They should be a clean, healthy pink; if not, your dog may have a serious disease. The following are some common signs of dental disease:

- bad breath
- bleeding
- change in eating habits
- difficulty in chewing
- pawing at the mouth
- reddened gums
- tartar buildup

How to Brush Your Chihuahua's Teeth

Before you begin brushing your Chihuahua's teeth, first familiarize him with the process. To this end, select a rubber finger brush that slides over your forefinger.

Don't worry about toothpaste yet—just massage his teeth with the finger brush. After a week or so of "pasteless brushing," add the toothpaste. Use a kind made just for dogs. (They come in a variety of flavors, including chicken, beef, mint, and peanut butter.) Dogs like meat-flavored toothpaste the best, of course. When you get good at pasteless brushing, it will take less than 30 seconds for the actual brushing.

If tartar is present, you can remove it with a tooth scaler. This is a simple process that any novice should be able to do. However, a tooth scaler probably will not be necessary if regular brushing is done. To remove tartar, simply place the scaler at the gum line, apply enough force to break the tartar free, and sweep the scaler toward the point of the tooth. A small amount of

Your Chihuahua needs an annual dental checkup and cleaning.

SENIOR DOG TIP

Grooming the Older Chihuahua

Grooming the older Chihuahua is a good time to check for lumps and tumor-type growths, because older dogs are prone to the development of these conditions.

Take some extra time to make grooming as comfortable as possible for your senior. This may require shorter grooming sessions, as well as allowing the dog to lie down. Also, instead of doing all grooming at one time, brush the teeth one day and trim the nails another. Finally, senior dogs may develop drier eyes as they age, so you may want to add a gentle eyewash designed for dogs to soothe and lubricate the eyes.

bleeding may occur during the process, but this is not a need for concern.

The Dog Dentist

Just as you need to go to the dentist for an annual dental checkup and cleaning, so does your dog. When a dog reaches the age of one year, have his teeth cleaned annually, and at six years, a twice yearly exam is best.

Dog dental care rivals the human kind nowadays. Canine dentists can do implants, braces, root canals, bonding, and even whitening. However, if you don't hold up your end by brushing your dog's teeth, all that fancy work will just go to waste.

Anal Sac Care

The anal sacs (often mistakenly called "glands") are two round organs located on each side of the anus (at the 4 and 8 o'clock positions). They exude powerful, bad-smelling secretions that are used to give other dogs mating and territorial information. Every time the dog defecates, some of this material is deposited. Dogs can also empty their sacs when they are scared or overexcited. A few dogs, however, have difficulty expressing these sacs on their own. Some people recommend routine emptying the anal sacs as a regular part of grooming, but this is not always a wise idea and can lead to further problems.

Dogs of all breeds and of any age may encounter anal sac problems. Anal sacs can become infected with bacteria (called anal sacculitis), become impacted or overfilled (which can lead to acute discomfort and infection), or develop tumors or foreign bodies. Signs that your dog is encountering anal sac problems include:

- chewing or licking the tail base
- clamping the tail down over the anus

- difficulty in passing feces
- redness or swelling in the area, perhaps even an open, draining sore
- reluctance to sit
- scooting his rear end along the ground

How to Express Your Chihuahua's Anal Sacs

You can learn to empty the sacs by holding a tissue against the anus on each side and squeezing the sac gently. Sometimes it takes several tries. If an impacted anal sac is not emptied, it can form an abscess and rupture out through the skin. This situation calls for veterinary treatment and a course of antibiotics.

Dogs with a history of anal sac problems may be candidates for having them surgically removed. Since your dog doesn't really "need" them, this is a pretty benign procedure, although you need to find a vet who is experienced with doing the operation. (A careless mistake could injure the sphincter muscles.)

Dog Attire and Accessories

The Chihuahua owner can satisfy any indulgence imaginable for her pet. In fact, dog attire and accessories run the gamut from complete matching clothing ensembles to extravagant toys and supplies.

Some Chihuahua owners feel that a sweater is essential once temperatures

FAMILY-FRIENDLY TIP

Children and Grooming

Children can assist with grooming in a variety of ways, depending on their age and maturity. Like routine care, though, grooming should not be left solely to a child. Children can be taught to brush a dog, help apply shampoo and cream rinse, and rinse the dog or hold a hair dryer, but all of these things should be done with adult supervision.

begin to fall. This is probably more critical for the smooth-coated Chihuahua than for the long coat. If you decide to dress your Chihuahua in a sweater, keep in mind that you're either going to have to wait until he has attained his full size, or you'll have to purchase a larger sweater once your puppy matures.

Once you have finished grooming your Chihuahua, a walk on lead or a treat will help him to remember the experience as a positive one. In fact, making the grooming experience a pleasant time will result in a dog who actually looks forward to this daily ritual.

Chapter 5

Feeling Good

Good health is the key to a good life, and many of the keys to health, including proper nutrition, exercise, and regular veterinary care, are in your hands. But even the dauntless Chihuahua may occasionally run into a spell of ill health. When that happens, the more you know and the more quickly you respond, the better the outcome will be. In this chapter, we'll take a look at some common health problems in the breed and discover what you can do about them.

Finding a Veterinarian

One of the biggest expenses you will encounter when it comes to your Chihuahua is the cost of veterinary care. However, the decision to bring a Chihuahua into your life should be made only after you know you can afford to take care of him the best that you can.

Selecting your Chihuahua's veterinarian is one of the most important things you will ever do for him. If you live near your Chihuahua's breeder, you may want to consider asking her which vet she recommends. I cannot emphasize enough how important this decision is—you should research potential vets as carefully as you would your own doctor.

Once you have decided upon a veterinarian for your Chihuahua, you should observe her manner and technique for the first few visits. You will be able to tell right away—from the time the vet takes your Chihuahua out of the crate and begins interacting with him—whether this person is right for your pet. A doctor who is truly in tune with small animals will not appear rushed. She will also know how to talk to and stroke your Chihuahua to relieve his anxiety.

Make sure that the examining room where your pet is to be seen appears clean and professional. Observe whether proper infection control is practiced by the vet and her staff. You do not know if the animal who was just

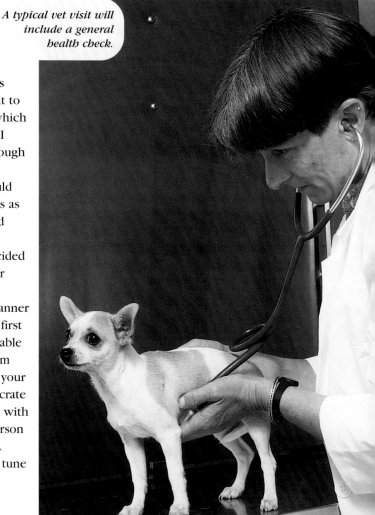

A typical vet visit will include a general health check.

treated in the next room had a contagious illness, for example, so you should observe thorough hand washing between exam rooms or the removal of soiled gloves, followed by hand washing and a clean pair of gloved hands for your pet's examination. Finally, although some veterinarians are not huge conversationalists, the one you choose should still share her findings with you and advise you what is best for the health of your Chihuahua.

The First Visit

Most veterinarians will ask that you bring in a fecal sample on your first visit, in order to test for the presence of intestinal parasites. If worms or worm eggs are found, medication will be prescribed to rid the digestive tract of these pests. If your pet is not already altered (spayed or castrated), the vet will probably recommend a time when this should be done. An important recommendation I would make for a first visit is that you consider having a microchip implanted in your dog for identification purposes. As discussed in Chapter 2, this permanent form of identification is highly effective in reuniting lost dogs with their owners.

The Annual Vet Visit

Your Chihuahua will need to see the vet for his annual physical examination. A typical visit will include a general health check, as well as the administration of booster vaccinations.

The Expert Knows

Small Dogs and Anesthesia

While no surgery is ever 100 percent safe, modern anesthesia is safer than ever. Toy breeds are at a somewhat higher risk during anesthesia because of their small size. However, modern drugs such as isoflurane are quite safe when administered by a properly qualified veterinarian.

Feeling Good

A rabies shot will be given if needed, depending on the laws governing your geographic area. Most schools of veterinary medicine have decided that annual boosters for canine diseases like distemper and parvovirus are not necessary if the initial injection was given after the puppy reached six months of age and met certain criteria. Discuss with your vet what her stance is on booster vaccinations.

The teeth should also be examined as part of this annual visit. If you have been diligent about brushing and scaling your pet's teeth, the finding should be a nice, clean mouth. If a buildup of tartar is found, you should expect your doctor to schedule a follow-up visit, at which time your Chihuahua will be put under anesthesia so that a complete cleaning can be done. Please discuss your vet's experience with the use of anesthesia on small dogs before your Chihuahua is put under.

Altering Your Chihuahua

Chihuahuas sold as pets are often altered (spayed or castrated) before they are sold. If they are not altered when they are sold, registration certificates may be held until documentation from a vet is presented that the pet is now altered.

Unless you have a show-quality dog whom you intend to breed, you should have your dog altered, and the sooner the better. Spaying and castrating is good for the community, good for you, and good for the dog.

Benefits for the Community

There are too many unwanted dogs in our society, and thousands of them are euthanized every year. Every dog should be a wanted dog.

Benefits for You

Altering is more convenient for you. Unspayed females experience heat cycles, and males fight with other males, mark in the house, and pester females. Unaltered dogs are also less focused on training. The longer you wait to alter your dog, the harder he or she will be to housetrain. Get it done before your dog is a year old, and the earlier you can do it, the better.

Benefits for the Dog

Perhaps the greatest advantage of altering is that your dog will benefit. Altered pets have twice the average life expectancy of unaltered pets, partly due to a much lower incidence of mammary, uterine, prostate, and testicular cancers.

The decision to breed your Chihuahua should be made only after considering the time, cost, and planning involved.

Vaccinations

Vaccinations work by "priming" your dog's immune system. They allow the immune system to proof itself against disease by going to work on dead or extremely weak viruses, so that when the "real thing" comes along, the immune system recognizes and destroys the invader before it has a chance to make your dog sick.

Just as with human beings, vaccinations are a critical part of your dog's health care—they save lives. Neglecting to vaccinate your dog puts him and others at serious risk of catching or transmitting communicable diseases. Not every dog requires every single vaccine, however. Consult with your veterinarian to determine what vaccines she recommends for your Chihuahua.

The following are some diseases against which dogs are commonly vaccinated.

Bordetellosis (Kennel Cough)

This coughing disease goes by a number of names, but the symptoms are the same: a coughing that sounds like your dog has something stuck in the back of his throat. In some cases, the cough is followed by retching. The disease is a highly contagious inflammation of the windpipe (trachea). It is most common in dogs who are housed in close quarters or who are boarded. There is

Vaccinations will help protect your Chihuahua against a variety of diseases.

no cure, but bordetellosis usually resolves itself in a couple of weeks.

Distemper

Canine distemper is a worldwide viral disease of dogs that affects many organs and systems of the body. It is also a highly contagious disease (related to human measles), and about half the dogs who get it will die. It is usually transmitted through contact with respiratory secretions. Puppies between three and six months of age are the most susceptible to distemper and also the most likely to die from it. Affected dogs have nasal and eye discharges, fluid loss, depression, dehydration, stumbling, seizures, and paralysis. No antiviral drugs exist that can cure the canine distemper virus, but there are excellent vaccinations to help prevent the disease.

Feeling Good

Leptospirosis

There are several kinds of leptospirosis bacteria, all of which are able to be passed on to humans. Dogs can contract the disease through exposure to the urine of an infected dog, rat, or wild animal. It affects the liver and kidneys. Dogs living in rural areas who are exposed to livestock are most at risk, so your Chihuahua may not require this vaccine.

Lyme Disease

Lyme disease is carried by ticks and causes lameness and arthritic-like symptoms in dogs. The vaccine is recommended only if your Chihuahua spends a lot of time in tick-infested areas, such as in the woods. Most infected dogs show no clinical signs, and the majority of dogs who contract Lyme disease readily respond to treatment with antibiotics.

Parvovirus

Parvovirus causes severe infection in puppies and dogs. It invades and destroys rapidly growing cells in the intestine, bone marrow, and lymphoid tissue. Its chief signs are nausea, vomiting, and severe, bloody diarrhea. This disease can be fatal, especially in puppies. There is no cure for parvovirus, only supportive care.

Rabies

Rabies is a deadly neurological viral disease that is transmitted through the bite of an infected animal. Puppies should be

Puppies are commonly born with roundworms.

immunized against it between 16 and 24 weeks of age.

Parasites

Parasites are little organisms that live on, or get their meals from, your dog. Some, like fleas and ticks, live outside your dog. Others, like worms, live inside. And mites live in a kind of half-and-half state—in the skin but not completely internal, either. Chihuahuas are more at risk from parasites because they are so small. In fact, a serious flea infestation can give your Chihuahua anemia!

Internal Parasites

The intestine is the commonest site of internal parasites, although some can infect other places, such as the heart or lungs. Many intestinal parasites can be transmitted by oral-fecal contact, and most internal parasites are diagnosed by microscopic examination of the feces for eggs released by the female in your pet's intestine. Your dog's feces should be checked for internal parasites twice a year.

Coccidia

Coccidia are protozoal parasites that infect mostly dogs and cats but can show up in other species. They have a complex life cycle that involves several developmental stages. Signs occur in young animals and include bloody diarrhea and abdominal pain. Diagnosis is made by identifying the tiny eggs in

Senior Dog Health

The decline in health of a senior Chihuahua is inevitable. Aging is often not pretty for humans, and the same is true for the Chihuahua. Help your dog age with dignity by respecting him and understanding that he may have some physical limitations.

Senior dogs have an increased chance of chronic illness, just as people do. The immune system starts to break down, joints get creaky, and the organs fail to work as efficiently as before. However, attention to diet and regular preventive veterinary care will keep your older friend in great health and good spirits for many years. This is one of the most long-lived of all dogs!

59

Feeling Good

a stool sample. Sulfa drugs or sulfa and antibiotic combinations are used to treat the infestation.

Giardia

Giardia is a waterborne parasite that lives in the small intestine; in fact, it is often found on fecal exams of apparently healthy dogs who have no signs of the illness. However, many vets recommend treating dogs who test positive for giardia, even if they have no outward signs of the disease.

Giardia attacks the intestinal tract, causing diarrhea, pain, and vomiting. A vaccine is available to protect your Chihuahua puppy from this infection.

Hookworms

Hookworms penetrate a dog's skin, are ingested as larvae, or are passed through the mother dog's placenta or milk. From there, they enter the small intestine, where they suck blood from the dog. Dogs, especially puppies, can get very sick from hookworms. Signs include bloody feces and colitis. Infected dogs might require hospitalization. Hookworm larvae can also penetrate the skin of human beings and cause significant irritation.

Heartworms

The heartworm is a potentially lethal internal parasite in dogs, and all it takes is one bite from a mosquito carrying a heartworm larva for a dog to become infected. Unfortunately, the dog doesn't usually show signs of heartworm infection until the later stages of the disease. Treatment is available, but it is risky. Prevention is a much better idea! However, even if your dog is on a regular heartworm preventive, testing for the disease should be performed every year, preferably before mosquito season.

Ringworm

Ringworm is not really a worm at all but a fungal infection primarily affecting young dogs. The fungi live in dead skin tissue, hair, and nails. Hair loss may occur, leaving a dry, crusty patch. The head and legs are the areas most commonly affected. Ringworm is treated by clipping the hair around the

Good medical care
will help prevent
disease in your
Chihuahua.

lesions and using an antifungal
shampoo or dip. Lime sulfur is used as
a topical treatment, and oral
medications may also be prescribed.
Ringworm is contagious to people and
other pets, so infected dogs need to be
kept away from children and other pets
until the infection is cured, which can
take two or three months.

Roundworms

One of the most commonly seen
intestinal parasites in dogs are
roundworms. They are long and round
and look like spaghetti. Puppies are
usually born with them. Common
symptoms in puppies include a
distended belly and diarrhea, and in
some cases, the roundworm will be

present in feces or vomit. Affected, well-cared-for adult dogs don't usually show any signs, although some may cough or have occasional vomiting. There are several effective treatments for roundworms, but the parasites can remain viable for a long time in the environment. Unfortunately, children are susceptible to infestation because of their tendency to put things in their mouths and their natural attraction toward puppies.

Tapeworms

In spite of their prevalence, tapeworms are not a significant cause of disease in dogs. The dog generally acquires these worms after swallowing fleas that carry the larvae. Most tapeworm segments look like grains of rice and are diagnosed when they are observed in the dog's feces or crawling around his anus. Several medications are highly effective in getting rid of them.

Fleas are directly responsible for the most common kind of tapeworm, so keeping your dog on flea prevention will solve the tapeworm problem, too. To avoid tapeworm infestation, control fleas and don't allow your dog to eat rodents.

Whipworms

Whipworms are not visible to the naked eye. The female whipworm lays eggs, which eventually turn into larvae, in the environment. Whipworms attach to the large intestine, or cecum (a sac where the small and large intestines meet). They usually affect dogs only. Signs of whipworm include chronic diarrhea, anemia, and weight loss. Several oral medications are used to treat whipworms, but their control is difficult, because the eggs in the environment are very resistant.

External Parasites

External parasites live on, rather than in, your dog. Most are bloodsuckers, but some ingest skin debris to survive.

Mites

Ear mites are tiny, crab-like parasites that live in the ear canals of dogs and cats. They cause severe itching and consequent scratching, as well as a bad odor. Any ear problems should be seen by your vet immediately for diagnosis and treatment.

Dogs can also be affected by two different kinds of mange mites. Demodectic mange is caused by a microscopic mite called *Demodex canis*. These mites live in the hair follicles, causing hair loss and red, thickened skin. Sarcoptic mange (scabies) is a highly contagious parasitic disease caused by the microscopic *Sarcoptes* mite.

Check your dog for fleas and ticks after he's been playing outside.

Fleas

Fleas are the most common external parasite. They feed on blood, which is bad enough, but when they bite, they inject their saliva into your dog's skin, causing itching in most dogs and allergic reactions in others. Fleas are easy to prevent through the application of one of many spot-on applications. Consult your veterinarian to determine which treatment is best for your Chihuahua.

Ticks

Ticks transmit many, many diseases, including Lyme disease, ehrlichiosis, Rocky Mountain spotted fever, and babesiosis. You don't want ticks around!

If you have seen ticks in your home, it's not a bad idea to apply flea and tick powder to places where the rug meets the wall around the entire room, as well as in obvious cracks. Wash your dog's bedding regularly as well. Removing leaves and clearing brush and tall grass from your property will help keep ticks away.

Fractures

Because Chihuahuas are fragile, they are prone to fractures. Never allow your Chihuahua to jump off high places or from your arms. In addition, the molera, that soft spot on the head that many Chihuahuas have, means that he may be more unprotected from trauma there than other breeds are.

Ticks are tough to kill, so the easiest way to keep them off your dog is by using a once-a-month topical insecticide. This is applied to a small area on the back of the pet, usually the back of the neck where he can't reach to lick at it. Always read and follow the directions carefully. Other choices include sprays, powders, dips, rinses, and collars. It's a good idea to ask your vet what she recommends. All tick-prevention products require that the tick actually be in contact with the active ingredient for it to have its effect. To maximize your dog's safety, examine him carefully after he has been outside.

Health Issues in Chihuahuas

The following are some health issues that may affect the Chihuahua. It's important to remember that although this may seem like a long list, most Chihuahuas will not develop any of them.

Cancer

Like other dog breeds, Chihuahuas can get cancer, although it is less common in them than in many other breeds.

Pet owners may first notice cancer as a visible lump; however, not all cancers form lumps, and not all lumps are cancers. If you notice a lump, your vet may extract cells from it with a syringe and evaluate them under a microscope, or she may remove the lump surgically and examine it. Removing lumps while they are still tiny reduces the chance of malignant tumors spreading. It also lessens postoperative discomfort as well as surgical cost and risk.

One kind of cancer that Chihuahuas do get is melanoma, usually starting when they are about eight or nine years of age. Some of these tumors are benign and others are malignant, but in all cases, they need immediate attention. The best treatment for melanoma is surgical excision of the tumor and the nearby surrounding tissue.

Collapsed Trachea

This is a condition characterized by a narrowing or collapse of the windpipe.

Signs may include wheezing, difficulty breathing, and a harsh, honking cough. Mild cases can be treated with cough suppressants. (Check with your vet before medicating your Chihuahua.) Also, reducing your Chihuahua's exertion may help treat the condition. Surgery may be necessary in more severe cases.

Cystinuria

This is a fancy name for the formation of cystine crystals in the urine, which eventually leads to kidney and bladder stones. Chihuahuas are at a higher-than-average risk for this condition. Signs include blood in the urine, pain when urinating, and having to urinate frequently, with only a small amount produced. If a stone completely obstructs the urethra, blocking the outflow (a condition more common in males), acute kidney failure may result. Treatment may include putting your Chihuahua on a special diet and increasing his water intake. Surgery is sometimes necessary.

Eye Conditions

The Chihuahua is prone to a variety of eye conditions, which are described in detail below.

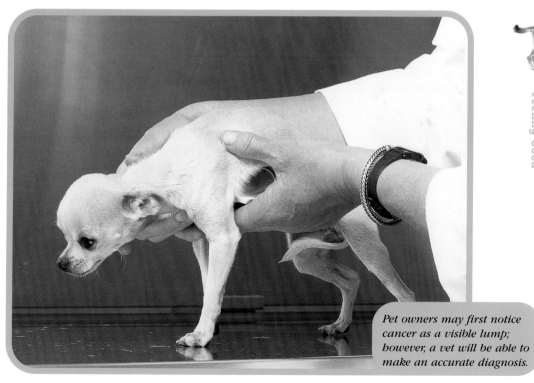

Pet owners may first notice cancer as a visible lump; however, a vet will be able to make an accurate diagnosis.

First-Aid Kit

Your canine first-aid kit should include the following items:

- 1-inch (2.54-cm) white tape and gauze tape
- balanced electrolyte fluid
- eyewash
- gloves
- hydrocortisone ointment
- hydrogen peroxide
- karo syrup
- oral syringes
- rolls of elastic wrap
- scissors
- styptic powder
- thermometer
- tweezers

Conjunctivitis

One common eye problem is conjunctivitis, an inflammation of the mucous membranes of the eye. Dogs with allergies are most susceptible. There may be a discharge as well. If your dog's eye looks red, take him to the vet to have it checked out.

Keratitis

Keratitis is another eye disease to which Chihuahuas are prone. In fact, Chihuahuas can get two types: One type is called chronic superficial keratitis, or degenerative pannus, and the other type is called keratoconjunctivitis sicca, or dry eye.

Degenerative pannus occurs mostly in German Shepherd Dogs but seems to be showing up more and more in Chihuahuas. It is not painful, but affected dogs can lose vision in the eye.

As the name suggests, dry eye occurs when there is insufficient moisture in the tear film. It is usually accompanied by a thick discharge. Treatment involves tear stimulants and anti-inflammatories.

Progressive Retinal Atrophy (PRA)

Progressive retinal atrophy (PRA) first shows up as a night blindness, with both eyes affected. Eventually, the dog becomes totally blind. A similar problem, called Central PRA or RPE dystrophy, is characterized by accumulations of pigment in the layer of pigmented lining of the retina. This also eventually results in total blindness. There is no cure for this condition.

Hypoglycemia (Low Blood Sugar)

Hypoglycemia is shared by many members of the toy breeds, who often do not have a sufficient reserve of fat around their liver. It is most often seen in young dogs and is, in fact, sometimes called juvenile hypoglycemia. Signs include lethargy, weakness, lack of coordination, and if not treated, coma or death. Emergency treatment is as simple as a little sugar in the form of honey, Karo syrup, or a commercial product that is especially formulated for pets. However, always follow up with a visit to your veterinarian.

Never feed your Chihuahua foods that are high in sugar, like candy, as a regular treat. This can cause his blood sugar to surge and then drop drastically, leading to a hypoglycemic episode.

Luxating Patellas

One condition that plagues this breed is a structural problem of unsound hind legs. You will hear the problem referred

Take your Chihuahua to the vet immediately if you suspect that he has an eye condition.

to either as slipped stifles or as luxating patellas. With this condition, the kneecap (patella) slips out of its groove and moves against the thighbone instead of along its natural groove. The tendency for the condition is inherited, but it can be aggravated when a small, active dog runs around and leaps off furniture. Signs include rear-leg lameness, shifting from one leg to another, hopping, or an inability to extend the leg completely. If left uncorrected, arthritis can result. A veterinarian experienced in toy breeds can diagnose the severity of the problem and recommend the best treatment, which often involves surgery.

Mitral Valve Disease

This term includes a number of cardiac conditions involving the

67

Feeling Good

Poisoning

Thousands of dogs are poisoned every year. The main causes of poisoning are pesticides, especially insecticides (usually through contact with the concentrated product); prescription drugs (even a Chihuahua can easily chew through a childproof container); over-the-counter medications (often given on purpose to pets under the mistaken belief that they will work on them just as they do with people); plants; and household cleaners like soaps and detergents. If you suspect that your dog has been poisoned, call your vet right away with as much of the following information as you know:

- name of the poison
- how much has been ingested or inhaled
- how long ago the poisoning occurred
- weight of the dog
- specific signs of poisoning, such as panting, vomiting, etc.

In an emergency, you can call the ASPCA Animal Poison Control Center. Located in Illinois, the specially trained staff provides assistance to pet owners and specific diagnostic and treatment recommendations to veterinarians 24 hours a day, 7 days a week. To reach the ASPCA Animal Poison Control Center, you can call the following numbers:

- (900) 443-0000. The charge is billed directly to the caller's phone.
- (888) 4ANI-HELP (888-426-4435). The charge is billed to the caller's credit card only.

degenerative thickening and progressive deformity of one or more heart valves. It is usually accompanied by a heart murmur that a vet will be able to detect upon examination. Males are more likely than females to be affected, and older dogs are the primary victims, although an occasional younger animal can also be diagnosed with the disease.

Signs of mitral valve disease include exercise intolerance, shortness of breath, weakness, fainting, and night coughing. There is no prevention for this condition. However, early detection and appropriate treatment may improve the prognosis and give your dog more years to live.

Pancreatitis

This disease is an inflammation of the pancreas. The disease may occur after your dog eats something he shouldn't (like garbage) or after eating too much fat. A dog with pancreatitis may experience lethargy, loss of appetite, vomiting, diarrhea, and abdominal pain. Pancreatitis is an emergency, so rush your Chihuahua to the vet immediately. The only treatment for the disease is supportive therapy, which usually includes feeding your dog intravenously for a few days in order to give his digestive system a rest.

Retained Baby Teeth

Sometimes a puppy may fail to shed his deciduous, or baby, teeth. This can obstruct and displace permanent teeth. Your veterinarian is also your dog's dentist, so she will be able to remove the retained teeth.

Skin Diseases

Skin diseases are common in dogs. While seldom fatal, they can be chronic nuisances to both dog and owner. Many cannot be cured, either, although most can be controlled with the proper treatment.

Skin problems can result from bacterial, fungal, allergic, or hormonal skin diseases. They can also be caused by parasites. Some are hereditary or result from a breakdown in the immune system. Because skin disease can have so many causes, it is imperative to have your dog checked by the vet to discover the cause and discuss possible treatments.

Baldness

Certain kinds of baldness occur as a hereditary condition in some Chihuahuas. One such type is pinnal alopecia, a condition in which hair loss begins at about six months of age and progresses to naked ears by eight or nine years of age. The exposed skin becomes black, while the rest of the coat appears normal. There is no treatment available for this condition.

Staph Infections

Staphylococcus ("Staph") is one of the most common bacterial skin diseases. It is not contagious to people or other pets. The disease causes itchy, crusty patches to form on the skin, especially on the chin (referred to as "chin acne"). It can be treated by shaving the hair away from the infected spot and treating it with an antibiotic ointment, as well as oral antibiotics, for three or four weeks.

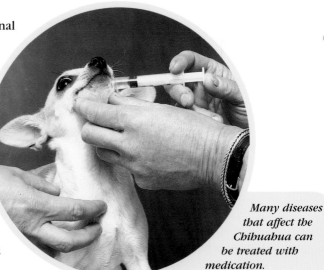

Many diseases that affect the Chihuahua can be treated with medication.

FAMILY-FRIENDLY TIP

Kids and the Vet

Talk to your child about what to expect at the vet's office. She should understand that the Chihuahua might cry out briefly if an injection or blood test is required but that he is not going to hurt for any long period of time.

One of the most important things to teach your child is that she should not pet any of the animals waiting in the office. Some of the animals could be quite sick with a contagious illness. Petting these animals and then petting the family Chihuahua is unwise from an infection control point of view. Also, animals, especially sick animals, are not always friendly and may not appreciate a child reaching out to them.

Yeast Infections

Another common condition in Chihuahuas is malassezia dermatitis, a yeast infection. On normal, healthy skin, yeast causes no problems, but when the environment of the skin is altered because of excess moisture or bacterial disease, malassezia can cause severe dermatitis (skin infection) or otitis (ear infection). The problem often begins in the summer, owing to the increase in humidity and to allergens in the air, but may persist throughout the winter. Malassezia ear or skin infections are very itchy and distressing to the dog. About half the dogs affected have underlying problems such as an allergy or an immune system problem that needs to be addressed. Once these are ruled out, the yeast can be treated with antifungal drugs and medicated shampoos.

Alternative Therapies

There is a wide array of alternative medicine available to your pet, including acupuncture, chiropractic, herbal therapies, and homeopathy. Keep in mind that not all alternative therapies are effective, and none should be considered a replacement for standard veterinary care.

Acupuncture

Acupuncture is the use of fine needles to stimulate the energy channels. No one is sure how it works, but many owners have found it useful to treat a variety of diseases, especially arthritis and similar problems. Only a qualified veterinary practitioner should perform veterinary acupuncture.

Chiropractic

Chiropractic care for animals is similar to that in humans and involves

A host of alternative therapies can complement traditional medicine, resulting in a healthier dog.

the manipulation of bones and joints. Only a qualified veterinary practitioner should perform chiropractic therapy.

Herbal Therapies

Herbs are strong medicine; in fact, many of the regular veterinary medicines used today have their origin in herbs. Just because they are "natural" does not make them safer than any other drug, though. In fact, herbs contain ingredients that can be dangerous in the wrong dose or if used for the wrong ailment. Never use herbs unless you are under the guidance of a qualified practitioner.

Homeopathy

Homeopathy involves the use of minute quantities of a curative substance (plant, animal, or mineral) that is then energized by dilution and shaking. This is a safe therapy, with anecdotal stories of success, but there is no peer-reviewed scientific literature that suggests it works better than a placebo.

Chihuahuas are healthy dogs who regularly live for 16 to 18 years. By making sure that your dog sees a vet regularly and receives good food and exercise, he'll be a joyful companion to you for every one of those years.

Chapter 6

Being Good

Rumors of how difficult the Chihuahua is to train abound, and while this may be true for some pet owners, these tales are much more the exception than the rule. However, Chihuahuas are not natural "obedience" dogs like Golden Retrievers are. They can be stubborn, manipulative, and difficult to housetrain—qualities that make it *essential* that you train your dog.

Positive Training

Chihuahuas are smart, sensitive animals who absolutely require gentle training techniques. This is sometimes called positive training, meaning that it is reward based. However, most good training involves at least a little "negative" training, too, such as telling a dog "no!" The key is to be gentle. Chihuahuas are fragile in spirit and in body, and they don't take kindly to being screamed at by a giant (you). Striking one of these tiny treasures is also absolutely out of the question. Gentle, firm, consistent training, on the other hand, will work wonders.

Socialization

The first step in good training is socialization, which simply refers to the ability of the dog to respond to and get along with humans and other dogs. Some dogs are fine with people but not other dogs (often the case with Chihuahuas). Others are good with other dogs but fear humans. And some, unfortunately, are terrified of everything.

How to Socialize Your Chihuahua

Because a Chihuahua is so small, the first step in implementing good socialization techniques is to make him feel safe. This includes curbing your kids or other dogs. A large dog or clumsy child could actually kill this little dog with frightening ease and without meaning to. Chihuahuas instinctively know this and tend to be shy around loud, fast-moving

Socialization is an integral part of the training process.

mammals like children and other dogs.

It is equally important to avoid spoiling a Chihuahua. It is tempting to want to become the all-protective parent, but this creates a dog who is frightened of the world—everybody but his owner, that is, whom he has wound tightly around his little paw.

With these things in mind, socialize your Chihuahua puppy as soon as he has visited the veterinarian and received his initial shots. I like to begin the socialization process by simply taking a new puppy outside and attaching a long, light leash to him and letting him explore the great outdoors. Allow your puppy to smell all the new smells he can find, and occasionally pick him up for some reassurance and bonding. Talking to the puppy at this time will allow him to learn the sound of your voice.

But your dog is going to need to get along with people other than yourself. To socialize your puppy to the human world, it's important to let him meet people in a safe setting. The more friendly people he meets, the more confident he will be. In fact, if your dog meets 100 people by the time he is four months old, you are well on the way to a well-adjusted Chihuahua. Men, women, babies, and

The Expert Knows

Treats

Rewarding your Chihuahua with treats for a job well done is a great way to positively reinforce a behavior. However, a treat should not be offered unless it has been earned. For example, if you are attempting to teach the *sit* command, do not offer the treat until your dog is actually in the sit position.

Experiment to see what treats your Chihuahua likes best, and try to have them on hand when training him. Make sure that the treats you offer are small in size and able to be chewed easily. Large, hard treats are not suitable for the tiny Chihuahua.

people in uniform, on bikes, and with canes should become "old hat" to your Chihuahua.

Crate Training

A comfortable crate is your Chihuahua's best friend. It is a den, a retreat, a traveling van, and a bedroom. When your Chihuahua is in his crate, he is not underfoot. He is safe from the vacuum cleaner, the visitors, and so forth. The crate is not a cage, because most dogs go into them willingly. In fact, most of the time, you can leave the door open. The crate should be a nice, warm,

Housetraining a Chihuahua requires patience and dedication.

quiet place where the puppy feels most secure; it should never be used as a place of punishment.

How to Crate Train Your Chihuahua

Nothing is simpler than crate training. You simply take advantage of a dog's natural need to den up during times of stress. You can make it super easy by luring your Chihuahua into the crate with bits of high-value treats like chicken or liver—or even feeding him in there. Before either of you know it, the den will become "home." It's a mobile home, too, by the way, so your dog can go with you and be safe wherever you are.

Housetraining

Chihuahuas are so tiny that they don't make much of a mess when they eliminate. That sounds like an advantage, but if you're not careful, you'll end up deciding it's easier to clean up after your dog than to bother housetraining him. At least that's, unfortunately, what many Chihuahua owners decide.

You can housetrain your Chihuahua, but it requires some patience. It's not unheard of for a Chihuahua to take one full year to become reliably housetrained. However, with the right training techniques, your Chihuahua will be on his way to better bladder and bowel control.

How to Housetrain Your Chihuahua

Puppies who are less than four months old should never be expected to remain in their crates for extended periods of time. This is because all puppies have weak sphincter control, and Chihuahuas in particular have tiny bladders. By the time your puppy is four months old, though, he should be able to go through the night in his crate without needing to go outside to eliminate, as long as you take him out right before you go to bed. A four-month-old puppy may still have the occasional accident, but he should be well on his way to becoming completely housetrained.

The main reason people fail at housetraining is because they are not consistent. They try one thing one day, decide it doesn't work, and then try something else. This confuses a dog. However, by developing a systematic approach to housetraining, you can make this difficult job a lot easier. This approach includes five steps: containment, resolve, attention, praise, and scheduling.

Step 1: Containment

A crate is a necessary tool when it comes to housetraining your Chihuahua. It is a portable home that helps him learn to confine his elimination activities to a suitable area—namely the outside world. The crate should be large enough for an

FAMILY-FRIENDLY TIP

Children and Training

Your child can be part of the training process. However, she should not be the only person involved. Even if your child is old enough to help out, total training responsibility should not fall to her.

adult Chihuahua to stand and turn around in. If you find yourself having problems because your puppy uses a corner of a too-large crate as a bathroom, you can buy dividers that will discourage this behavior.

Keep in mind that very few dogs can bear to soil their own bedding. This is not because it smells bad to them but because it leaves them vulnerable—an odiferous signal to the world that they are nearby. Dogs like to leave their mark on places they visit, but they prefer to keep their sleeping places, where they are more vulnerable, secret. Of course, a dog who is crated too long will fail at housetraining, no matter how perfect the crate size is or how much he wants to succeed.

If your puppy uses his crate for a bathroom even though you give him plenty of outdoor opportunity and watch for every signal he gives, it's possible that the bedding is too absorbent and comfortable—in other words, too great a temptation. Try replacing, at least temporarily, that cushy bedding with something a bit more understated, like newspaper, and see if the problem improves.

Step 2: Resolve

It is important that you be patient with your Chihuahua when it comes to housetraining. Most dogs are not completely housetrained until they are three to four months old, and Chihuahuas often take longer. Their bladders are small and their sphincters are insufficiently developed before that time to be able to "hold it."

When a dog makes a mistake in the house, he doesn't mean to annoy you, to soil his home, or to create a mess. Dogs make messes because they either do not understand what you want or because they can't control their behavior yet.

When your Chihuahua eliminates in the proper place, be sure to praise him effusively.

Step 3: Attention

Paying attention to your dog really means two things: observation and supervision. You need to do both well and consistently if you hope to housetrain your Chihuahua.

Your Chihuahua may be giving you subtle signs that he needs to

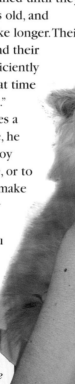

Use treats to positively reinforce your dog for a job well done.

eliminate, and you may miss these signs because you're not paying close enough attention. Watch your puppy like a hawk. Young puppies do not usually march to the door, whine or bark loudly, and sit politely until you finish reading the comics. In reality, he may not make any noise at all. He may circle, look worried, stare at you, lick his lips or paws, or wander near the door.

It's up to you to learn to read your Chihuahua's signals. Once you understand them, you must respond immediately. Go out *with* your dog; don't just let him out. Stay with him the entire time. If you're out there with him, you can see what he's doing. Your company will also make your puppy feel less like he's being exiled. If you just put him out and leave him there alone, he'll assume that he is being punished.

Some people have a lot of success tethering their dog to themselves while working on housetraining. To use this method, tie your dog loosely to you while going about your daily tasks. Here you accomplish a number of things:

- You are "containing" him.
- You are bonding with him.
- You are giving him exercise.
- You are paying attention to him.

Step 4: Praise

Once your puppy does the right thing, praise him wildly. A mere pat on the head and a subdued "good boy" is not sufficient. Chihuahuas expect you to show true joy, even ecstasy, in their accomplishment. You must show this joy by delightedly jumping up and down, offering food treats, and effusively praising him. Wait until your puppy completes eliminating before you praise him, though. If you praise him too early, you'll interrupt his train of thought (so to speak), and he may not finish. Timing is everything!

Punishment, on the other hand, never works at all. Even a comparatively mild punishment, like shaking a finger at the dog's nose, can facilitate a snapping response. Even if you catch your Chihuahua in the house right in the middle of the act, don't punish him. Don't scream or yell "NO," and don't rub his nose in it. Instead, carry him out the door, if possible. Dogs are less apt to continue urinating while being carried, so with any luck, you can get him to finish his business outdoors, where you should praise him extravagantly for finishing.

Step 5: Scheduling

Keep your young Chihuahua on a strict schedule. Take him out within a few minutes after eating and right away after he plays or sleeps. If you are gone all day, don't expect your puppy to "hold it." You probably can't do that yourself, and it's so unfair to expect it of a puppy. Ideally, a young Chihuahua should be taken out on a leash to eliminate every two hours for the first two or three weeks you have him. That is the only way you can prevent him from making a mistake.

If you are gone all day, you must do one of the following:

- Come home for lunch and a nice walk. This will give you both a break and help you to keep your puppy on a housetraining schedule.

Basic obedience training will result in a well-mannered pet.

- Get a dog-walker or a kind neighbor to come over to walk your dog during the day. You can water their plants in return.
- Take your Chihuahua to a dog day-care center. These facilities are springing up all over the country, and they provide your dog with companionship as well as potty breaks.
- Install a dog door. Even a reluctant Chihuahua can learn to use one in a couple of hours. Don't shove your Chihuahua through the door, though; you'll only frighten him. Lure him with treats, and he'll soon get the hang of the thing. Of course, dog doors can be used safely only in connection with a secure backyard.

If any of this sounds expensive or like too much work, remember that it's nothing compared with the time and expense of replacing your carpets every month.

Accidents

If your Chihuahua accidentally eliminates inside the house, clean up the mess quickly and completely. Blotting the spot where your puppy has urinated may dry it, but the scent will remain, prompting your dog to eliminate there again. Because urine contains lots of ammonia, using a white vinegar spray to neutralize the ammonia smell often works well. A well-formed bowel movement can be picked up with a bit of toilet tissue. Here again, some sort of disinfectant to mask the odor is essential. To actually get rid of the odor, rather than just mask it, you need to resort to the use of an enzyme cleaner.

Basic Commands

Teaching a puppy the most basic commands should happen after fundamental lessons like socialization, crate training, and housetraining are well on their way to being learned.

Your Chihuahua should be a mannerly household pet. A trained dog is a pleasure to be around and will be included more often in activities than will an ill-trained dog. Good training can also save your dog's life.

Sit

The *sit* command is easy to teach, but it is

The *Down-Stay*

In formal obedience classes, your Chihuahua may learn a long *down-stay*, which usually lasts for a couple of minutes. This command is a combination of the *down* and the *stay*.

often used inappropriately—usually when the owner really wants the dog to stay still, get out of the way, or not make a nuisance of himself. The catchall "sit, boy" is supposed to magically cure all the bad habits your dog has gotten himself into. It doesn't, of course, and it's much better to work on actually curing your dog's bad habits (like jumping up) than to tell him to sit every time he does them. The *sit* is a useful command, of course. I ask my dogs to sit before I give them a treat, because it's easier for me to find their little mouths that way. It's also useful as a prelude to nail clipping. And it's a simple trick for children to practice with the family dog. But it's no substitute for good all-around behavior.

How to Teach Sit

The easiest way to teach the *sit* is to say "sit" in a cheerful voice while holding a tiny (pea-size) treat over your Chihuahua's head, gently curving the treat backward over his head. Most dogs will sit naturally. If your Chihuahua does sit, praise him and give him the treat. Do not force him into the *sit*—gently encourage him. If he gets up too quickly, refrain from treating him. He needs to learn that the treat comes only when he is actually sitting. Otherwise, you'll turn him into a jack-in-the-box.

Stay

Some people teach the *stay* as a separate command from the *sit*. I believe that teaching the *stay* as a separate command is confusing to dogs, because you're not asking them to do anything new—you're just asking them to keep doing what you have already asked them to do. However, other people believe that saying "stay" signals to the dog early that he'll be sitting for quite some time. At any rate, never ask your dog to sit-stay for more than a few seconds when you are starting out. You want to make success easy for him.

How to Teach Stay

Teach the *stay* by saying the word and then gradually retreating. Reward your Chihuahua for staying in one place. Again, quit while the training is still fun. The length of time you teach this command depends on your individual dog, but five minutes is usually long enough.

Down

Most dogs dislike being asked to lie down, although they are happy enough to do it on their own. This is because the *down* puts them in a vulnerable position, both physically and psychologically.

How to Teach Down

To teach the *down*, use the treat method again. While the dog is sitting, lower the treat slowly, and move it toward the floor. Most dogs will lie down naturally. If yours doesn't after a few tries, you can gently extend his front legs and praise him as you ease him to the floor. Don't push down on your Chihuahua's shoulders to force him down; you can actually dislocate his shoulder in trying to coerce him. Besides, you already know you're stronger than he is. You want him to perform joyfully, not out of fear or pain.

Come

Teaching your Chihuahua to respond to your command to come is the most important lesson of all. To help your dog succeed with this command, you must make him realize that you are the source of the treats, the petting, the praise, and the fun.

How to Teach Come

To teach your Chihuahua to come, attach a leash to your dog and choose a room that is small enough not to tempt him to

Your Chihuahua's leash is literally his line of communication with you.

Training the Older Dog

Older dogs *can* learn new tricks. It may take a bit longer for your older dog to bond with you, but once the bonding is in place, pleasing you will become his top priority.

When training your senior, be sure to motivate him with lots of praise and rewards, just as you would with a puppy. Also, keep in mind that there may be some issues that need to be resolved with an older dog before you can engage in rigorous training. Take him to the vet for a complete physical examination, as health problems or behavioral issues can interfere with the training process.

Patience is required when training your senior Chihuahua, but your efforts will be rewarded as long as your expectations are realistic.

a dog, this is a more inviting stance.

Next, call him gently, and offer him a treat. Chances are he'll toddle over. Praise him with every step. If he doesn't come, softly draw the leash toward you, still encouraging him. Don't tug or yank—the purpose of the leash is to help him focus. The ideal situation is that your Chihuahua never realizes it's even thinkable to go in a different direction than the one you're calling him to. When he responds by taking some steps in the right direction, praise him, and be sure to treat him when he reaches you.

Dogs are extremely good at reading body language, so make sure that your posture, your tone of voice, and your commands are all saying the same thing. If you angrily call your dog to come while standing in a stiff, off-putting posture with your arms folded, your dog is reading the message behind the words—you're mad, and he won't want to come to you. Likewise, be careful about calling your dog to come to you for unpleasant procedures. What sensible creature would come to his owner to be punished, medicated, or given a bath?

Practice the *come* command several times a day. When your Chihuahua gets really good at this (at least two weeks of perfect behavior), experiment off lead in a secure area. Also, in the beginning, don't practice in times of high excitement or lots of distractions. Your dog won't be able to concentrate,

run off. Kneel so that you are close to his level, and extend your hand. You might also open your arms in an inviting, sweeping gesture. Do not lean toward the dog, but lean away from him. Put your body at an angle to his, because to and that will guarantee a failure. It's all a matter of simple psychology. You need to be more interesting to your dog than anything else.

Heel

The leash is your dog's lifeline. It is not only his protection, but it's his line of communication (literally) with you when you are out on the town. Don't think of the leash as a restraining device; think of it as a way to stay close to your dog. With only a little encouragement, your Chihuahua will look forward happily to the sight of the leash being taken off its hook—it means walk time.

Because Chihuahuas are tiny, you'd think it would be easy to teach them to walk calmly on lead. And it's really not very hard, although you'd never know it by the alarmingly large number of Chihuahua owners you see permanently entangled by their own leashes while their Chihuahuas dart merrily all around them.

How to Teach Heel

Begin your work with your Chihuahua when he is on lead, not free. He should be responding to the *come* command before you start teaching him to heel (which means to walk nicely on lead at your heel). Enforce your command, if necessary, by kneeling and using a treat to lure your dog, but don't pull him. Use the leash only to keep him from going in the other direction.

It is customary to have the dog walk on your left side. It doesn't really matter, but if you plan to engage in formal obedience training, you might as well start getting into correct practice right away. Start by keeping a little treat in your left hand. The point is to get your Chihuahua to believe that staying close to that appendage is likely to yield its rewards. Because a Chihuahua is pretty low to the ground, though, it's important to bend down when you feed him. You don't want to get him in the habit of jumping up for the treat.

Treat your dog frequently as you

Trick training is a great way to build on simple obedience commands.

direction—just don't respond to it. Stay still or move in a different way. Soon he'll realize that all the rewards come from staying near you.

After your Chihuahua becomes accustomed to walking on the leash and you don't have to give him a treat every two seconds for walking politely, ask him to sit when you stop. Reward him when he does. Soon your Chihuahua will sit calmly by your side whenever you stop to chat with friends. If you do not want your Chihuahua to sit

walk along but only when he's in the correct *heel* position. To help position your dog, hold the leash behind your thigh. Start walking in a counterclockwise circle. Since your dog will be the inside, you'll find it easier to guide him as you move along. Say "Rover, heel!" in a happy voice, and start walking. Don't scold him if he goes in the wrong

automatically at every stop, make sure that you say "sit" before you give him a treat.

Don't make every walk a lesson. Allow your Chihuahua plenty of time to snoop around and check things out, especially when you begin your walk. It may be exasperating to you, but Chihuahuas really enjoy this part of the adventure. You can signal to your dog that a certain part of the walk is his turn to lead by using some special command (whatever you like) and loosening up on the leash. I say "you lead!" and start following him.

Teaching Tricks

Now that your dog knows the basics, it's time to teach him some tricks. Trick training is really no different from regular training. The "trick" is patience, treats, ending on a positive note, and practicing only five minutes at a time. Soon your Chihuahua will know the tricks so well that your friends and family will be extremely impressed.

Spin

This one is a real crowd pleaser and so easy to teach! Have your dog stand in front of you, and hold out a really special treat in your closed fist. Lead in him a gentle circle and say "spin! spin!" When he completes a circle, let him have the treat. Praise him lavishly and repeat the whole process. Practice every day for a few minutes until you feel comfortable just having him follow your finger. Give him the treat afterward. Soon enough, you can just "spin" your finger, and your dog will follow.

Shake

Another simple trick you can build on is "shake." Say "shake," and take your dog's paw. Then, give him a treat. Repeat until your dog figures out that

when you take his paw, it means that a treat is on the way. Soon he will volunteer his paw.

To build on the trick, try teaching the "wave." Say "shake" as usual, but this time hold your hand just out of reach. As your dog raises his paw in an attempt to meet your hand, say "wave!" and hand him the treat. Repeat until he seems to have it figured out. Soon he'll be able to differentiate "shake" from "wave" both by your verbal command and how you hold your hand.

A trained dog is charming, easy to get along with, and a pleasure to own. Fortunately, a determined, kind, fair-minded owner can make almost any Chihuahua into a great pet.

Chapter 7

In the
Doghouse

A puppy is a commitment for the long haul. Unfortunately, many puppies end up in animal shelters seeking adoption simply because their owners did not want to keep their commitment, especially when negative behaviors like excessive barking, chewing, digging, housesoiling, jumping up, and nipping became problematic.

Every new puppy owner will face some, if not all, of these issues to varying degrees. However, with a little patience and training, your Chihuahua's behavior should improve.

Barking

You must decide how much barking you want to tolerate and set this limit from the first time your Chihuahua begins yapping. This breed will bark at suspicious strangers, which in a Chihuahua's mind include guests, other dogs, letter carriers, and passersby. And while all dogs bark, excessive barking drives everybody but the dog crazy.

Solution

For many people, about six warning barks are enough. At that point, pick your dog up, say "Rover,

that's enough," in a calm voice, and place your hand gently over his muzzle. Then put him down. It is important for him to understand that it is *you* who gets to decide which company are welcome guests and which are not. If he barks again, place him in another area (not his crate, which shouldn't be used as a place of punishment), and don't respond to the barking. When your dog has not barked for a few minutes, praise him quietly and allow him to rejoin the family or guests.

Keep in mind that dogs also bark because they are sad or lonely. If your Chihuahua is barking because he's been relegated to the backyard, just bring him in. It's what he wants, what he needs, and what he deserves. If your neighbors tell you that he barks all day when he is alone, he may be suffering from separation anxiety. In that case, you will

Barking is a dog's natural way of communicating.

need to address that issue first; the barking will stop of its own accord.

Chewing

Chewing is normal behavior for a dog and should be expected at all stages of your Chihuahua's life, especially in puppies. Chewing is the way that dogs explore their world. It is your job to make sure that what your dog chews is a safe dog toy and not an electrical cord.

Solution

If your Chihuahua latches onto a forbidden item, take it gently away, saying "No chew!" in a firm voice. Then, give him a suitable chew toy in return. The item that you choose should be easily distinguishable (even for the dog) from forbidden items. Thus, you can't give him an old sock to chew on and expect him to stay away from your good socks.

Because chewing is a natural behavior for your dog, you have to remove as many temptations as possible. If your shoes are in the closet where they belong and your Chihuahua's toys are in plain view, he'll go for the toys. The attraction to your shoes and dirty laundry is probably that your scent is on them. If there are things in the house that you can't easily move out of your Chihuahua's reach, spray them with a dog-aversion spray.

Besides normal, exploratory chewing, some dogs chew when they are bored or anxious. Here the

Finding a Behaviorist

If your Chihuahua exhibits problem behaviors, you will need to look for a behaviorist or experienced trainer to deal with them. While a veterinary behaviorist is your best option, certified ones are hard to find, although some general vets do specialize in treating behavioral problems without being certified veterinary behaviorists. Your best bet is to talk to your vet first to make sure that your Chihuahua's problem behavior is not caused by a medical problem. If a medical issue has been ruled out, ask your vet to suggest someone who is experienced in dealing with problem behaviors.

Interview a potential trainer and observe her behavior with your dog. Ask the trainer for her credentials and professional affiliations. Don't choose anyone who is rough or who arouses bad feelings in your dog or you. Sometimes you have to trust your instincts.

In the Doghouse

solution is not merely to hand them another chew toy but to address the problem that produces the anxious behavior. Dogs require company, for instance, and if you are gone all day, your dog has few options. You might consider getting a dog walker or sending your dog to puppy day care. This will give him something to think

All dogs have a tendency to dig from time to time.

about besides where your socks are. Some dogs appreciate having company, like another Chihuahua or a cat, but others prefer being the only pet.

Digging

While Chihuahuas are not out-of-control diggers like terriers and Huskies, they *are* dogs, and all dogs have a propensity to dig from time to time. Digging a nice hole in the soft earth is a way to get warm in the winter and cool in the summer. It may be a way to escape or a way to pass the time when bored. Some dogs even apparently dig in imitation of their owner's gardening efforts.

Solution

If your dog digs because he's bored, bring him into the house. If he's too hot or too cold, he also probably needs to come in. However, if he is digging just for the fun of it, you can try making him a nice soft earthbox. Let him watch you bury a couple of treats in it, and he'll soon figure out that the earthbox is by far the most rewarding place in the yard to dig. If you see your dog digging somewhere else, cry out "Look, Rover! Over here!" and race toward the earthbox.

Housesoiling

Housesoiling, or inappropriate elimination, is usually the product of allowing a puppy too much freedom too soon, not taking him outside on a regular schedule to relieve himself, or feeding him at irregular times. At the same time, puppies can have a hard time controlling their bladder—they can urinate simply because they are excited to see you. It is also possible, especially in a previously housetrained dog, that there is a medical reason for the behavior. Take your dog to the vet before assuming that he is being disobedient. Having said this, I must confess that Chihuahuas really hate the rain and cold, and they may have a dismaying tendency to choose convenience (for them) over good manners at times like this.

Solution

The first thing you should do to prevent housesoiling is to make sure that your Chihuahua is reliably crate trained. (See Chapter 6.) By their very nature, dogs dislike soiling their "dens," so the crate, provided it is small enough so that he can't "get away from it," makes it unlikely that he will soil his "bedroom."

If housesoiling continues to occur

Separation Anxiety

If you suspect that your Chihuahua is suffering from separation anxiety, seek professional help. This is a serious behavior, so it is crucial that you find someone who is well versed in this area. Remember that although a dog may not be the center of your life, you are certainly the center of his. A lonely dog can become stressed, despondent, and destructive. While some dogs seem to manage well enough by themselves, most dogs need companionship—preferably yours. If that is not possible, adding another dog (or even a cat) to the family can soothe anxious moments. Dogs from shelters who have experienced abandonment suffer most.

Drug therapy is a new and promising treatment for severe separation anxiety in dogs. But before medicating your pet, see what behavior modifications you can make in your own lifestyle. Luckily, neither you nor your dog has to suffer through separation anxiety. Treatment, both medical and behavioral, is available.

93

despite your best efforts, there is still hope. First, carefully evaluate when the housesoiling presents itself. If it happens, for example, as soon as your puppy leaves his crate on his way outside, next time try carrying the crate outdoors (with your Chihuahua still inside) before you let him out to eliminate. This will set your puppy up for success by not allowing him the opportunity to make a mistake in the first place.

Chihuahuas

The Lost Dog

Losing a dog is a heartrending occurrence for humans and dangerous to dogs. The best way to get a lost pet back is to make sure that he has visible identification. Statistically, it has been found that most dogs with an identification tag are returned to their owners, while most who don't have one are not. You have many choices in visible identification. Probably the most visible and simplest is an embroidered nylon mesh collar. You can have your dog's name and your telephone number embroidered on it, or if you prefer, just your telephone number. An identification collar takes away the worry of your dog losing his tags, something that happens all too frequently. However, since some dogs inevitably lose their collars as well, I suggest a backup method of identification, like tattooing, or even better, microchipping.

If your dog does become lost, put up color photos of your pet all around the area from which he disappeared. Offer a reward. Look everywhere for your dog. Think about how he behaves off lead—does he tend to charge off in a straight line, or does he wander around sniffing? Your Chihuahua will probably not have traveled too far from your house in the first 24 hours, so scour the area. Pay kids to help, and offer a bonus if they find the dog. If your dog is shy, tell them to try not to grab him but just to call you immediately.

Go to the animal shelter in person to see if your dog is there. If you just call, they might automatically tell you that he's not there, without even bothering to check. It's up to you to keep checking every day.

If your puppy urinates inside the house when he is overly excited, stay calm yourself. Don't greet him wildly, don't stare at him, and don't punish him if he makes a mistake. Excited urination usually occurs only in puppies who have poor sphincter control. It will generally cure itself. Submissive urination, on the other hand, happens when a dog is fearful. Just stay calm, ignore it, and pretty soon he will figure out that there is nothing to worry about and he'll stop the behavior. Punishing the behavior will only make your dog even more nervous.

Never shake or hit your puppy if he has an accident, and never rub his nose in it, either. These methods are cruel, and they will only make your dog afraid of

FAMILY-FRIENDLY TIP

Children and Aggressive Dogs

If your Chihuahua exhibits any kind of aggressive behavior, such as growling, snarling, or biting, do not allow him near your children until the problem is solved. To that end, it is important that you consult a trained behaviorist.

you. Watching your Chihuahua's behavior, training him to a crate, and

To prevent housesoiling make sure that your dog is reliably crate trained.

SENIOR DOG TIP

Training the Older Dog With a Problem Behavior

If you adopt an older Chihuahua, he may come with a problem behavior or two. Therefore, you will need to be consistent and firm with your training, just as you would be with a new puppy.

Barking, in particular, is among the most difficult habits to deal with and one of the most common issues seen in dogs, including older dogs. Knowing when and why your older dog barks is critical to solving the problem. For example, an older dog who was never around small children may bark if he is suddenly exposed to them. Patiently allowing for bonding between your older pet and your child will help alleviate some of the barking. However, your dog should never be expected to accept your child without carefully established interventions. Placing your older dog on your lap and inviting your child to sit beside you while you are stroking and reassuring the dog is a good icebreaker. Once you feel your Chihuahua relax, you can suggest that your child also stroke him gently. I would suggest keeping your hand on your pet at the same time that this is going on, and closely observing your Chihuahua's reaction to the child. Hopefully, desensitizing your dog to your child will help relieve the excessive barking when she is present.

In general, older pets should not be significantly harder to manage than puppies if you are patient and firm but positive with your training.

keeping him on a rigid feeding schedule are the best ways to keep your dog from eliminating inappropriately.

Jumping Up

Luckily, a jumping Chihuahua is not the danger or annoyance that a jumping St. Bernard is. Perhaps because of this, though, people tend to simply allow the behavior to continue. They even reward it by saying, "Oh, you little cutie!" and scooping the dog up in their arms.

Solution

If you don't want your Chihuahua jumping up on you, simply don't reward the behavior. Don't look at or speak to him—just walk away. When your dog is quiet and standing with all four feet on the floor, crouch down close to him, and pet him quietly. Soon he will figure out that quiet behavior on his part will be rewarded with attention on your part.

Nipping

Nobody likes getting nipped or bitten, even by a Chihuahua. Puppy teeth are extremely sharp, partly to compensate for the lack of jaw power and partly to ensure the weaning process.

Solution

The best way to stop nipping is to never allow it to get started in the first place. Dog teeth do not belong on human skin, period. Your puppy can easily learn what is called "bite inhibition" if you scream, cry out, and cease playing with him the minute that he nips. He will soon learn that nipping results in the loss of playtime.

If you feel that the nipping is not in play but is a result of aggression, it is best to talk with an experienced trainer about what issues you may be facing. Most biting occurs because the dog is stressed or fearful, or in some cases because the dog feels that a little aggression on his part will make him ruler of his world. Aggression in Chihuahuas can be solved if the whole family is dedicated to the task. However, professional advice is usually required.

It is important to remember that what seems like bad behavior to you is either natural behavior for a dog or else his way of trying to cope with what to him is an intolerable situation. If you keep thinking like a dog and looking at the problem from his point of view, you'll be surprised to discover how many creative solutions you can find.

Teach your puppy bite inhibition by crying out when he nips.

Chapter 8

Stepping Out

Once your Chihuahua is trained, you will probably wonder what new challenges and activities the two of you can undertake together. Well, rest assured—there is a nearly endless list of possibilities! Before you "take the plunge" into any of the ventures described in this chapter, though, do your research and obtain as much information as possible. The Internet and your Chihuahua's breeder are two good sources to start with.

Traveling With Your Chihuahua

Because the Chihuahua is so small, he can be included in your travel plans with only a few limitations. Common sense rules out taking your pet into a crowded place where he can easily be stepped on, for example. Taking a trip with your Chihuahua can be a rewarding experience, but just remember that you are an ambassador for the breed when you travel, so make sure that both you and your pet mind your manners. And don't forget to have a good time!

Car Travel

Car travel should be routine for your Chihuahua, and most of these dogs love to travel. If yours doesn't, it may be because he fears the destination. If the only time he gets a ride is when he is going to the vet, for example, you can expect trouble. If this is the case with your dog, make trips a joy for him by taking short journeys to fun places. Take him to the park or even to a new block for his daily walk. He'll be thrilled; it doesn't take much to impress a dog.

Of course, you are responsible for your dog's safety while en route. Your Chihuahua should be safely restrained in a safety seat made for dogs. You wouldn't take a drive without your seatbelt, so give your Chihuahua the same advantage.

Whatever device you use to restrain your dog, the safest place for him is the back seat. Even a restrained dog can be killed by an airbag. (A device unsafe for someone as large as a 12-year-old child is not safe for a Chihuahua.) Also, never let your dog hang his head out the window, even in the rare instances when he can reach up to do it, since grit and other debris can get lodged in the eye.

The tiny, portable Chihuahua can be included in many of your travel plans.

Air Travel

Air travel can be stressful for dogs, so try not to fly with your Chihuahua if at all possible. I would never put my dog on a plane unless he is going to travel with me under the seat. If you absolutely must fly with your dog and can't sit with him, call the airline for the latest information.

In general, it is best to book a direct, midweek flight or one with only one stop. In the summer, select an early-morning or late-evening flight. Your dog will need to be in a crate that is:

- Large enough to allow a dog to stand, turn, and lie down in a stretched-out position.
- Sturdy, without interior protrusions. It must have handles or grips.
- Leak-proof on the bottom and lined with plenty of absorbent material.
- Ventilated on opposite sides, with exterior rims or knobs to prevent blocked airflow.
- Labeled "Live Animal" in large letters, with arrows indicating the upright position, and your name, address, and phone number.

Except on the advice of your veterinarian, don't tranquilize or sedate your dog before flying with him. This kind of medication can interfere with his heat regulatory system.

Packing for Your Pet

When traveling with your Chihuahua, you should always pack a crate, exercise pen, first-aid kit for dogs, food and water dishes, the food your dog normally eats, leash, newspapers, shampoo, towels, treats, and trash bags. You may also want to consider bringing water from home for your dog to drink, as some animals' digestive systems may not react well to different regional water.

Accommodations

One of the reasons that dogs cause trouble when traveling is that their much-beloved routine has been shattered. Your Chihuahua is in a new place, with strange things happening and strange people all around. He may get unsettled, nervous, or downright scared. If you have to leave him alone for any length of time, he might also get bored. All of these factors can add up to trouble.

Rules vary from place to place, but basic etiquette does not. Do not attempt to sneak your dog into an

FAMILY-FRIENDLY TIP

Traveling With Your Dog and Child

When traveling with your Chihuahua and child, make sure that your child respects the dog's space. This can be a stressful time for your pet, so it's important that he be made as comfortable as possible, not teased or annoyed. Making sure that your child has enough to keep her busy on a long car ride will make the journey an enjoyable one for all parties involved.

establishment, and always clean up after him and respect all rules regarding animals. Most motels will not allow you to bathe your pet in their bathtub or sink. They also may require your dog to be crated when you are gone.

Keep your dog clean and well brushed. The more you brush him outside, the less he'll shed inside. And that's good news to the people who have to clean the room. Remember, you don't want dogs to get a bad name.

Sports and Organized Activities

Your Chihuahua should already know his basic commands, so perhaps a sport or organized activity is the next adventure upon which to embark together.

Agility

Agility is an organized activity that requires a dog to complete a timed obstacle course as quickly as possible. The course contains obstacles such as weave poles, jumps, and a tunnel—all things that a Chihuahua can do very well.

If you think that you might enjoy agility, go and observe a competition to see if it is something that you would like to do. Also, make sure that you assess your Chihuahua's personality; a happy, outgoing dog who is afraid of nothing is the ideal candidate for agility competition. However, remember that Chihuahuas are fragile dogs, and jumping from high places can be injurious to them. Practice agility only with a mentor.

Obedience

It is the rare Chihuahua who excels at obedience, as they have a definite mind of their own. However, that just makes this activity more of a challenge. Who wants a push-button dog, anyway?

In an obedience event, a dog must qualify with a score of 170 out of a perfect 200 points, plus earn at least half the points possible for each exercise at one of three levels: Novice,

Open, or Utility. In Novice, the dog must heel on lead for a figure eight, stand for examination, heel off lead, recall, and do a long *sit* and long *down*. Titles offered in obedience include Companion Dog (CD), Companion Dog Excellent (CDX), Utility Dog (UD), and Utility Dog Excellent (UDX).

A new kind of obedience is becoming popular—rally obedience, known affectionately as rally-o by its supporters. Rally-o combines classic obedience with the more exciting elements of agility. In addition, rally-o handlers are free to talk to and praise their dogs in ways that are disallowed in classical obedience. This is a really enjoyable event for exhibitors and spectators alike.

Showing (Conformation)

A conformation show is a beauty contest, where a dog is judged against the breed standard. The goal is for a dog to win his "championship," which means earning 15 "points." One to five points are

Traveling With an Older Dog

When traveling with your older Chihuahua, keep in mind that he may need to stop more often to eliminate. In fact, if he has trouble urinating at home, know that this issue will still be a problem when traveling. An older pet may also be stiff when he is allowed to leave his crate, so you should respect his need for a bit of extra time at each rest stop.

awarded to the best male and female Chihuahuas of each coat type in the show, and a dog must win under at least three different judges. At least two of the shows have to be "majors" (shows worth three or more points), which means that your dog is facing a lot of competition.

There are a variety of classes you can enter at a dog show. Long- and smooth-coated varieties are shown separately, in each gender. There are special classes for

Agility requires a dog to complete a timed obstacle course as quickly as possible.

Sports and Safety

puppies, novice dogs, American-bred dogs, bred-by-exhibitor dogs, and "open" dogs, which is a kind of free-for-all. However, which class you should enter is a matter of some strategy, and you will succeed in the show ring only if you find a mentor, an experienced Chihuahua person who can guide you through the dog-show jungle. Join your local kennel club, and discover the joys of dog showing.

When you purchased your Chihuahua, you chose either a pet-quality or a show-quality dog. If you purchased a pet-quality Chihuahua, more than likely, he lacks some important characteristic that is necessary in a show dog. If you are thinking of entering a dog show with a Chihuahua whom you purchased as a pet, go to the breeder and tell her of

your plan. A responsible breeder will be able to discuss the breed standard with you and help you to make a decision. Sometimes puppies sold as pets do mature into much better adults than the breeder felt possible. This is a rare occurrence, but it does happen, especially with Chihuahuas who were purchased at a very young age.

If you purchased a show-quality Chihuahua, a responsible breeder will coach you through the training process and be able to advise you when your pet is actually ready to enter his first show.

Games

The creative mind can come up with all sorts of games and activities for the Chihuahua.

Because of his small size, though, there are limits to what kinds of games are safe for your dog. An example is that of flying disk. Larger dogs will run and leap high into the air to catch the disk, but unless your Chihuahua far exceeds the average breed size, flying disk is probably not the best game for him.

Some basic games, like fetch or tug-of-war, require little equipment and are sources of great enjoyment for both the Chihuahua and his human companion.

Fetch

While a Chihuahua is not a retrieving dog, he can nonetheless learn to fetch. Not only is fetch a great way to bond

In a conformation show, a Chihuahua is judged against the standard for the breed.

with your pet, but it also offers needed exercise. Exercise makes dogs tired, and tired dogs make happy owners.

One way to get started is to use two identical toys. Throw the first. Your dog will probably naturally run after it. When he gets to it, call him and show him that you have another toy—he'll probably run back. With luck, he'll carry the first toy with him. Then, throw the second toy. You may have to go back to retrieve the first toy yourself, but pretty soon, your dog will catch on. And if he doesn't, at least you'll get some exercise yourself.

Tug-of-War

Everybody knows how to play tug-of-war, but how many people get to play it with a Chihuahua? They are stronger than they look, but not much. Thus, you need to be gentle, and you should never let a child play tug-of-war with the family Chihuahua. Your dog could get hurt.

Showing is fun. Agility is fun. Even obedience can be fun. But Chihuahuas are much more than show or obedience dogs. They are the smallest and most charming members of the family. They will put up with being shown, being told to sit and stay, and even fetching balls (small ones) for you. But they much prefer a cozy evening by the fire, sitting on your lap, or taking a cheerful stroll with you wherever you go.

Resources

Associations and Organizations

Breed Clubs

American Kennel Club (AKC)
5580 Centerview Drive
Raleigh, NC 27606
Telephone: (919) 233-9767
Fax: (919) 233-3627
E-mail: info@akc.org
www.akc.org

Canadian Kennel Club (CKC)
89 Skyway Avenue, Suite 100
Etobicoke, Ontario M9W 6R4
Telephone: (416) 675-5511
Fax: (416) 675-6506
E-mail: information@ckc.ca
www.ckc.ca

Federation Cynologique Internationale (FCI)
Secretariat General de la FCI
Place Albert 1er, 13
B – 6530 Thuin
Belqique
www.fci.be

The Kennel Club
1 Clarges Street
London
W1J 8AB
Telephone: 0870 606 6750
Fax: 0207 518 1058
www.the-kennel-club.org.uk

United Kennel Club (UKC)
100 E. Kilgore Road
Kalamazoo, MI 49002-5584
Telephone: (269) 343-9020
Fax: (269) 343-7037
E-mail: pbickell@ukcdogs.com
www.ukcdogs.com

Pet Sitters

National Association of Professional Pet Sitters
15000 Commerce Parkway, Suite C
Mt. Laurel, New Jersey 08054
Telephone: (856) 439-0324
Fax: (856) 439-0525
E-mail: napps@ahint.com
www.petsitters.org

Pet Sitters International
201 East King Street
King, NC 27021-9161
Telephone: (336) 983-9222
Fax: (336) 983-5266
E-mail: info@petsit.com
www.petsit.com

Rescue Organizations and Animal Welfare Groups

American Humane Association (AHA)
63 Inverness Drive East
Englewood, CO 80112
Telephone: (303) 792-9900
Fax: 792-5333
www.americanhumane.org

American Society for the Prevention of Cruelty to Animals (ASPCA)
424 E. 92nd Street
New York, NY 10128-6804
Telephone: (212) 876-7700
www.aspca.org

Royal Society for the Prevention of Cruelty to Animals (RSPCA)
Telephone: 0870 3335 999
Fax: 0870 7530 284
www.rspca.org.uk

The Humane Society of the United States (HSUS)
2100 L Street, NW
Washington DC 20037
Telephone: (202) 452-1100
www.hsus.org

Sports

International Agility Link (IAL)
Global Administrator: Steve Drinkwater
E-mail: yunde@powerup.au
www.agilityclick.com/~ial

North American Flyball Association
www.flyball.org
1400 West Devon Avenue #512
Chicago, IL 6066
800-318-6312

World Canine Freestyle Organization
P.O. Box 350122
Brooklyn, NY 11235-2525
Telephone: (718) 332-8336
www.worldcaninefreestyle.org

Therapy

Delta Society
875 124th Ave NE, Suite 101
Bellevue, WA 98005
Telephone: (425) 226-7357
Fax: (425) 235-1076
E-mail: info@deltasociety.org
www.deltasociety.org

Therapy Dogs Incorporated
PO Box 5868
Cheyenne, WY 82003
Telephone: (877) 843-7364
E-mail: therdog@sisna.com
www.therapydogs.com

Therapy Dogs International (TDI)
88 Bartley Road
Flanders, NJ 07836

Telephone: (973) 252-9800
Fax: (973) 252-7171
E-mail: tdi@gti.net
www.tdi-dog.org

Training

Association of Pet Dog Trainers (APDT)
150 Executive Center Drive Box 35
Greenville, SC 29615
Telephone: (800) PET-DOGS
Fax: (864) 331-0767
E-mail: information@apdt.com
www.apdt.com

National Association of Dog Obedience Instructors (NADOI)
PMB 369
729 Grapevine Hwy.
Hurst, TX 76054-2085
www.nadoi.org

Veterinary and Health Resources

American Animal Hospital Association (AAHA)
P.O. Box 150899
Denver, CO 80215-0899
Telephone: (303) 986-2800
Fax: (303) 986-1700
E-mail: info@aahanet.org
www.aahanet.org/index.cfm

American Holistic Veterinary Medical Association (AHVMA)
2218 Old Emmorton Road
Bel Air, MD 21015
Telephone: (410) 569-0795
Fax: (410) 569-2346
E-mail: office@ahvma.org
www.ahvma.org

American Veterinary Medical Association (AVMA)
1931 North Meacham Road – Suite 100
Schaumburg, IL 60173
Telephone: (847) 925-8070
Fax: (847) 925-1329
E-mail: avmainfo@avma.org
www.avma.org

ASPCA Animal Poison Control Center
1717 South Philo Road, Suite 36
Urbana, IL 61802
Telephone: (888) 426-4435
www.aspca.org

British Veterinary Association (BVA)
7 Mansfield Street
London
W1G 9NQ
Telephone: 020 7636 6541
Fax: 020 7436 2970
E-mail: bvahq@bva.co.uk
www.bva.co.uk

Publications

Books

Anderson, Teoti. *The Super Simple Guide to Housetraining*. Neptune City: TFH Publications, 2004.

Gagne, Tammy. *The Chihuahua*. Neptune City: T.F.H. Publications, 2005.

Morgan, Diane. *Good Dogkeeping*. Neptune City: TFH Publications, 2005.

Magazines

AKC Family Dog
American Kennel Club
260 Madison Avenue
New York, NY 10016
Telephone: (800) 490-5675
E-mail: familydog@akc.org
www.akc.org/pubs/familydog

AKC Gazette
American Kennel Club
260 Madison Avenue
New York, NY 10016
Telephone: (800) 533-7323
E-mail: gazette@akc.org
www.akc.org/pubs/gazette

Dog & Kennel
Pet Publishing, Inc.
7-L Dundas Circle
Greensboro, NC 27407
Telephone: (336) 292-4272
Fax: (336) 292-4272
E-mail: info@petpublishing.com
www.dogandkennel.com

Dog Fancy
Subscription Department
P.O. Box 53264
Boulder, CO 80322-3264
Telephone: (800) 365-4421
E-mail: barkback@dogfancy.com
www.dogfancy.com

Dogs Monthly
Ascot House
High Street, Ascot,
Berkshire SL5 7JG
United Kingdom
Telephone: 0870 730 8433
Fax: 0870 730 8431
E-mail: admin@rtc-associates.freeserve.co.uk
www.corsini.co.uk/dogsmonthly

Index

Note: Boldface numbers indicate illustrations.

111

Index

Dedication

I would like to dedicate this effort to my family. My wife, Martha, and our children, J. Eric and Sarah, have supported me in my experiences with dogs. Our extended family now includes our daughter in-law, Tristin, and our son in-law, Roger. They, as well as our three grandsons, Konnor, Calvin, and A.J., are supportive to the greatest extent possible.

Acknowledgements

I cannot possibly name all the people who have encouraged, helped, critiqued, and advised me along my path. These people range from breeders, to judges, to teachers and mentors, to doctors of veterinary medicine, to professional handlers, to close friends both in and out of dogs, and kennel help that has allowed me to be away from home, knowing full well that my dogs are in good care. A value cannot be assigned to the contribution each has made; however, I feel a HUGE debt of gratitude to all these people.

About the Authors

Richard Miller is a well-known Chihuahua breeder and judge. He breeds and shows his Chihuahuas under the kennel name Mar-Rich. Mr. Miller has produced group winners, national specialty winners, and a variety winner at the Westminster Kennel Club Dog Show. Mr. Miller is approved to judge all toys, all non-sporting breeds, three hounds, three terriers, Best in Show, junior showmanship, and miscellaneous class. He lives in Illinois with his family.

Diane Morgan has authored numerous books on canine care and nutrition and has also written many dog breed and horse books. Diane lives in Williamsport, Maryland.

Photo Credits

Paulette Braun: 11, 21, 100, 103
Mike Ludkowski (Shutterstock): front cover photo
Chit Kit Sen (Shutterstock): 4
Lisa F. Young (Shutterstock): 19
All other photos courtesy of Isabelle Francais and T.F.H. archives.